TWO DIALOGUES

TWO DIALOGUES:

CONTAINING A COMPARATIVE VIEW OF THE LIVES, CHARACTERS, AND WRITINGS OF

PHILIP, THE LATE EARL OF CHESTERFIELD

AND

DR. SAMUEL JOHNSON
(1787)

BY

WILLIAM HAYLEY

A FACSIMILE REPRODUCTION

WITH AN INTRODUCTION

BY

ROBERT E. KELLEY

GAINESVILLE, FLORIDA

SCHOLARS' FACSIMILES & REPRINTS

1970

SCHOLARS' FACSIMILES & REPRINTS

1605 N.W. 14TH AVENUE

GAINESVILLE, FLORIDA, 32601, U.S.A.

HARRY R. WARFEL, GENERAL EDITOR

REPRODUCED FROM A COPY IN

AND WITH THE PERMISSION OF

YALE UNIVERSITY LIBRARY

L.C. CATALOG CARD NUMBER: 71-122486
ISBN 8201-1080-9

MANUFACTURED IN THE U.S.A.

INTRODUCTION

When in 1787 Thomas Cadell published William Hayley's *Two Dialogues; Containing a Comparative View of the Lives, Characters, and Writings, of Philip, the Late Earl of Chesterfield, and Dr. Samuel Johnson,* the artistic and, more important, the moral principles which purportedly guided biographers were causes of widespread disagreement. As always, practice outran theory. The last quarter of the eighteenth century is known less for the systematic promulgation of biographical *dicta* than for its readiness to engage in almost endless and often vitriolic controversies over individual biographies. These skirmishes were waged over a variety of questions: How fully should a biographer expose his subject's private life, his weaknesses, strengths, secrets, idiosyncrasies? Should he be ruled by principles of decorum, or is his primary duty to the revelation of fact, no matter how unpleasant, and to the curiosity of the public? How long after his subject's death should a biographer wait before issuing his work? How detailed should his book be? Other questions, of course, regarding biography were—and still are—asked, but the foregoing specify those which most concerned writers of the eighteenth century.

In publishing the *Dialogues* when he did, Hayley joined a succession of opportunists. Johnson had died in December, 1784, eleven years after Chesterfield. Between 1785 and 1788 appeared many pamphlets, sermons, reflections, poems, Boswell's *Journal of a Tour to the Hebrides*—a trial balloon for his *Life of Johnson*—and no fewer than five full-length biographies, including the disputed lives by Mrs. Piozzi and Sir John Hawkins. Apart from Mrs. Piozzi's edition of Johnson's letters (1788), Hayley's *Dialogues* was the last substantial piece of Johnsoniana to appear before the publication of Boswell's biography in 1791. This flood of materials about Johnson inspired numerous attacks in the press against his so-called "friends" who, it was widely felt, had "murdered" his reputation by publishing intimate accounts of his life and career.

But William Hayley (1745-1820) was a man oblivious to the fear of journalistic recrimination. While still young, Hayley retired to Eartham, Sussex, to devote his life to study, writing, gardening, and architecture. He soon became known as the "Hermit of Eartham" and even signed his letters "Hermit." Because he worked hard at being a literary man and managed to cultivate friendships with prominent persons, such as Anna Seward, George Romney, John Flaxman, Charlotte Smith, William Blake, William Cowper, and Edward Gibbon, Hayley made Eartham a retreat for writers and artists. Cowper spent some of his happiest days there. Gibbon, a frequent visitor, called Eartham an "earthly paradise."

Despite his good intentions and high aspirations, Hayley has never lived down his reputation as a man who seldom profited from his own experience. In the nineteenth century he was deprecated in Blake's acid epigrams, Byron's lines in *English Bards and Scotch Reviewers,* Gilchrist's biography of Blake, and Swinburne's essay on Blake. He was repeatedly scored for his lack of humor, his romantic temperament which precluded self-awareness, and his dilettantish ways. On the other hand, he did not lack close friends. William Mason, who published Hayley's last three books, named a son after him. In his biography of Cowper, Robert Southey defended Hayley, praising his delightful conversation, friendly heart, and winning manners. And, later in the century, Samuel Rogers remarked that "if Hayley was formerly over-rated, he is now undervalued." Despite such protests on his behalf, Hayley survives, somewhat unjustly, as a rather absurd figure. Most recently, Richard D. Altick expresses a general attitude when he describes Hayley as "the most laughed-at British man of letters of his time."

Hayley's chief aim was to write for the benefit of mankind. He allegedly helped cure Gibbon of gout by reading him some of his own poetry, and his *Triumphs of Temper* (1781), so a mother wrote him, caused her daughter's transformation from an intractable to a docile girl. These are the only published instances of Hayley's achieving his literary goals. His attempts at drama failed, and *The Triumphs of Temper,* written, according to Southey, to reveal "the various effects of spleen on the female character," was his major poetic success. Hayley's three verse essays, on history (dedicated to Gibbon), on painting (to Romney), and on epic poetry (to Mason), published in 1781 and 1782, reveal sound scholarship and a perceptive critical view. In 1790, at the peak of his literary career, Hayley was offered the laureateship, but, preferring a life of retirement, he declined. Hayley's verse remains almost unknown to modern readers, but there can be little doubt that it enjoyed the respect of many of his contemporaries.

Although Hayley continued to write verse until shortly before his death, from the mid-1780's onward, he devoted his main energy to prose. Most noteworthy among his prose compositions are his biographies of Milton (1796; first published in abridged form in 1794), of Cowper (1803-1804), and of Romney (1809). The last was denounced by Romney's son, the Rev. John Romney, in his *Memoirs of the Life and Writings of George Romney* (1830). He also wrote a memoir of his natural son, Thomas Alphonso, who died before he could fulfill his promise as a sculptor. This book was appended to the second volume of his autobiography, *Memoirs of the Life and Writings of William Hayley, Esq.*, written in the third person and published posthumously in 1823.

Historians of biography, if they mention Hayley at all, do so in unflattering terms. Writing to Cowper on February 7, 1792, Hayley promises that his biography of Milton would be "more candid" than earlier lives of the poet. This claim was to go largely unacknowledged, for the biography of Milton, since its first publication, has been ridiculed as sheer eulogy. Even so, Hayley's apology for panegyric in the *Life of Milton* is worth attending because it illustrates a concept of biography prominent in the age: "Biographers are frequently accused of being influenced by affection for their subject; to a certain degree it is right that they should be so; for what is biography in its fairest point of view? a tribute paid by justice and esteem to genius and to virtue; and never is this tribute more pleasing or more profitable to mankind, than when it is liberally paid, with all the fervor and fidelity of friendship: the chief delight and the chief utility that arises from this attractive branch of literature consists in the affectionate interest, which it displays and communicates in favour of the talents and probity that it aspires to celebrate."

It was the "fervor and fidelity of friendship" which led Hayley to produce for William Cowper a biography which, though still panegyric, was superior to the life of Milton. Hayley wrote this book, as he confessed in his *Memoirs*, to make Cowper "more known" and "more beloved." In order to fulfill this self-imposed obligation, he was forced to "sink in tender silence," as he put it, when dealing with the delicate matter of Cowper's mental aberrations. Although the prevailing taste of the age promoted such discretion in biography, Hayley's reticence on the subject was prompted chiefly by the pious urgings of Lady Hesketh, Cowper's cousin, who pushed Hayley in the direction of vagueness and euphemism. Hayley's major contribution in this work was his inclusion of a large number of Cowper's letters, a device which he admits obtaining from William Mason's *Memoirs of the Life and Writings of Mr. [Thomas] Gray* (1775).

When writing the *Dialogues*, Hayley was free of the influence of "friendship." There is no evidence that he was personally acquainted with either Chesterfield or Johnson or that he had more than the remotest association with members of their circles.

The *Dialogues* was published about July, 1787, some months after Hayley had circulated the work in manuscript among friendly critics. In his Memoirs he acknowledged that the work proved unpopular; nevertheless, it was reissued from Cadell's folded sheets in 1800 with a cancelled title by A. Cleugh, a distributor of popular and scandalous literature. If, in fact, the

Dialogues did enjoy notoriety, the reasons are certainly more obscure now than they may have been at the time of its publication. That Hayley was not confident of its success is perhaps evident because, contrary to his usual practice, he instructed Cadell to publish the book anonymously. The only other work to be issued without his name on the title-page was the *Essay on Old Maids* (1785), which annoyed many feminine readers. Hayley, in addition, was probably aware that the deprecation of Johnson's biographers had become the sport of the London press.

In writing the *Dialogues,* Hayley may have had in mind William Crawford's *Remarks on the Late Earl of Chesterfield's "Letters to His Son"* (1776), a series of eight righteous dialogues written to counter the influence of Chesterfield's *Letters to His Son* (1773). But it is clear that the main precedent for his use of the dialogue form is Plutarch's construction of parallel lives, a device widely imitated in the eighteenth century as a means of simplifying and telescoping contrasting lives and careers of famous persons. Actually Hayley's organization is less rigid than Plutarch's. The debaters roam rather haphazardly about, abruptly abandoning topics under discussion only to return to them later. This is clearly an attempt to make the *Dialogues* appear realistic by approximating the meandering quality of conversation.

Apart from any purely literary influence, it was natural for Hayley to capitalize on the famous antagonism of such eminent figures as Johnson and Chesterfield. After the publication of his letters, Chesterfield was generally vilified as the great enemy of morality. His name became a byword for pomposity, heartlessness, and shallowness. He was reproached as a man

Introduction

without allegiance to virtue, truth, religion, and morality. The aristocratic bias of his writing alienated many readers. But as his biographers have carefully shown, Chesterfield was a man of considerable charm, wit, kindness, perception, and good sense, whose letters, far from condoning or promoting deceit and adultery, were filled with warnings against drunkenness, profligacy, gluttony, and other social vices. The public was also inclined to forget the valuable government services Chesterfield performed as Lord Lieutenant of Ireland and Secretary of State. But contemporary moralists persisted in casting abuse on the *Letters.* Samuel Foote ridiculed him in his play, *The Cozeners,* and such lesser writers as Thomas Hunter, Jackson Pratt, and William Crawford, mentioned above, fulminated against him. In 1788, Chesterfield figured in another dialogue, *Curious Particulars and Genuine Anecdotes Respecting the Late Lord Chesterfield and David Hume, Esq.,* possibly by Samuel Pratt. Cowper satirized him in *The Progress of Error,* and, nearly seventy years after Chesterfield's death, Dickens caricatured him as Sir John Chester in *Barnaby Rudge.*

Samuel Johnson, on the other hand, was regarded as the moral and social antithesis of Chesterfield. Forgetting that Chesterfield and Johnson shared such attributes as good sense and seriousness, the public was eager to contrast Chesterfield's aristocratic reserve and worldly wisdom with Johnson's warmth of heart, appealing idiosyncracies, and sturdy devotion to truth. Johnson, too, had his enemies, and like Chesterfield, he fell victim to scurrilous abuse. But in comparisons between the two men, Johnson won the applause.

Long before Hayley wrote the *Dialogues,* the differences between the two men had been exaggerated. The numerous printed accounts, many of them by Johnson's early biographers, of the famous quarrel over Chesterfield's alleged refusal to aid Johnson in his work on the *Dictionary* sided almost unanimously with Johnson and used Chesterfield as an example of the faithlessness and meanness that pervaded the literary world. Modern biographers have done much to correct this distortion. Johnson himself was not blind to Chesterfield's virtues, once remarking that he was pleased with his Lordship's elegant manner and breadth of knowledge. Although he said that Chesterfield's *Letters* "taught the morals of a whore, and the manners of a dancing master," Johnson also thought them a "very pretty book," which, without what he regarded as their immorality, could be recommended for every young gentleman. Chesterfield, for his part, admired Johnson's famous letter of rebuke for its cogency and placed it on his table for all to read.

Hayley's *Dialogues* is interesting, however, because it is more than a mere fleshing out of the famous anecdotes surrounding the Johnson-Chesterfield debacle. Indeed, Hayley almost ignores the quarrel. Though not by any means a full-length biography, the *Dialogues* is considerably more than a random collection of memorabilia.

Hayley took pains to establish the authenticity of his piece. Borrowing a technique from the dedications and prefaces to many contemporary novels, he composed an "advertisement by the Editor" which claims that the *Dialogues* is a genuine document written by "Edmund," a student at Cambridge. "Edmund," in turn, wrote an "Introductory Letter" explaining that the *Dialogues* is

Introduction xiii

a sort of school-exercise debate and detailing the circumstances surrounding its composition.

Despite its relaxed prose, the "Letter" is an important illustration of Hayley's thoughts on biography. He seems, for example, less disposed to discretion than his later biographies indicate. He argues that because both subjects are dead the public has a right to "scrutinize, to estimate, and enforce their respective claims to immortality," and that qualified persons may voice their opinions of the two men. Hayley chooses not to write self-censored biography because, he says, it is too restrictive in its demands for accuracy and consistency, whereas he prefers "spirit and freedom" over a "few grains of logic." Thus by casting his piece in the mold of a fictional exchange of views between two educated men, an Archdeacon and a Colonel, he purchases greater freedom of movement and tone than if he had written in an established biographical mode. The very nature of the *Dialogues* is, in other words, a convenient escape clause. To illustrate, "Edmund" warns that each advocate tends to be overindulgent in defending his hero and in attacking his hero's rival. Exaggerated positions, it seems, are inevitable in such confrontations. In biography, such excesses are flaws. But the fictional debate enables Hayley to forestall charges of prejudice, for the author cannot be held accountable for the speakers' indiscreet remarks and outrageous judgments, or for the colorful figurative language which punctuates the debate.

The organization of the *Dialogues*, as agreed upon by the Archdeacon and the Colonel in consultation with Lady Caroline, the chorus-like arbiter, is rudimentary. The first dialogue focuses on Johnson, the second on Chesterfield. Each dialogue is ostensibly divided into two sections, the first dealing with the subject as moralist, the second with the subject as writer. Each of the two figures is to be granted equal time. The first dialogue, however, is nearly twice as long as the second. Furthermore, the difficulty of separating Johnson's and Chesterfield's careers into two such convenient categories becomes clear as the contestants repeatedly veer back into moral considerations after brief excursions into literary issues.

Within this framework nothing more than commonplace opinions are offered by the Archdeacon and the Colonel. Neither new information nor original views about Johnson and Chesterfield are introduced. The Archdeacon's defense of Johnson as a self-made man and writer, practical moralist, devout Christian, and learned writer, and his attack on Chesterfield as a man who, in his life and writings, scorned decency and promoted vice, merely echo contemporary sentiment. Similarly, the Colonel's shrill declamations against Johnson's religious superstition, melancholy, social brutality, and ponderous writings, and his support of Chesterfield as a man whose career and writings had been grossly misunderstood and unjustly maligned, hardly break new ground.

We cannot, therefore, look to either speaker for consistent and logical justifications of their heroes' reputations. Despite repeated disclaimers of partiality, the Archdeacon and especially the Colonel constantly allow themselves hyperbolic accusations and defenses. But the exchange between them works to Hayley's advantage, since he can offer opposing attitudes towards Johnson and Chesterfield without having to choose between them, a tactic which becomes important when certain delicate areas such as the "dark hints" of Johnson's early life come under discussion. In these instances Hayley, through innuendo without explicit condemnation, can introduce controversial matter without risking charges of indiscretion. Thus, Hayley's use of the dialogue frees him from the necessity of drawing firm conclusions about men whose complex and often misunderstood personalities prompted mixed emotions among the public at large.

The *Dialogues* has sometimes been described as thoroughly anti-Johnson in its bias. Sir Joshua Reynolds, who composed two brief dialogues in imitation of Johnson's conversational style, was offended by Hayley's treatment of his friend, saying that Hayley distorted Johnson's true character by relating anecdotes which revealed his distasteful idiosyncrasies. Mrs. Rose thought the *Dialogues* "more distinguished for malignity than wit." Boswell ignored it. The *Monthly Review* (LXVII [December 1787], 457-459), while praising Hayley's "elegance and spirit," scorned the *Dialogues* as merely another mockery of Johnson's memory. On the other hand, the *Scots Magazine* (XLIX [September 1787], 451-452) and the *Gentleman's Magazine* (LVII [June, July 1787], 520-521, 612-614) commended the work. Mrs. Elizabeth Montague, Queen of the Bluestockings, also approved the *Dialogues*, but for precisely those reasons which excited condemnation, namely, its supposed injustice to Johnson. So well known was her antipathy to Johnson that she was suspected by some of being the author.

There is external evidence to suggest that the *Dialogues* was composed partly out of Hayley's pique at being informed of Johnson's contempt for *The Triumphs of Temper*. Mrs. Rose says that in revenge Hayley ridiculed Johnson in the character of Rumble in his play, *The Mausoleum* (1784). He also took exception in his life of Milton to Johnson's strictures on the poetry of Milton and Thomas Gray. Hayley's only modern biographer, Morchard Bishop, agrees that the *Dialogues* paints an unfavorable portrait of Johnson and argues that Hayley's attitude towards Johnson was influenced by his friend, Anna Seward, Johnson's townswoman and life-long enemy. An exchange of letters between Hayley and the Swan of Lichfield, as Anna Seward was called, printed in the *Gentleman's Magazine* (LXIII [March 1793], 197-199), attests to the correspondents' delight in berating Johnson.

Nevertheless, not all of the evidence points in this direction. In the first place, the *Dialogues* is by no means written to bolster Chesterfield's reputation at the expense of Johnson's. It is doubtful that the Colonel is intended to serve as Hayley's spokesman, for his extreme assertions about both subjects can scarcely be regarded as definitive. Moreover, Hayley's choice of a clergyman as Johnson's defender suggests a moral sanction of Johnson's life and career. Likewise, Lady Caroline's placing two volumes of Johnson's writings on top of a volume of Chesterfield's works in order to provoke the debate is a foreshadowing of the verdict. The Archdeacon is quick to notice this point, saying that the position of the books "hit my fancy as an emblem of justice. . . . I represented to my imagination the decisive triumph of the once indigent and neglected, but truly great Moralist, over the highborn and fashionable Wit, whose vain talents were, during his life, the idol of his country." Ultimately Hayley implies victory for the Archdeacon, a victory confirmed in rather comic fashion when, at the close of the first dialogue, the Colonel is suddenly converted to the Archdeacon's viewpoint.

The *Dialogues* is not, however, merely a synoptic account of the careers of two eminent and controversial individuals. It is significant because it is a reduction of a biographer's impulses to commemoration and to malice. Biographies designed to commemorate or to annihilate the memories of famous men abound in the eighteenth century, as in every age. Hayley offers, however, alternative views of Johnson and Chesterfield so as, in the long run, to mitigate their differences. At the conclusion, the general impression left is that the stridence which marks the *Dialogues* is muted in favor of more reasonable evaluation of Johnson and Chesterfield. The Archdeacon and the Colonel may be regarded as symbols of the contrary temptations which beset every biographer—the desire to construct a narrative of an appealing, exemplary life and the impulse towards scandal-mongering. In this way, the arguments of these two debaters embody the biographer's obligation to weigh and sift evidence as he tries to evaluate his subject, as he tries to reconcile his subject's virtues and weaknesses in order to present a balanced estimate. The biographer must first compose all available evidence, however conflicting, before he reaches his judgments. But the dialogue form enables Hayley to evaluate and reach at least tentative conclusions at the same time. Lady Caroline is given the final word. She is speaking of Johnson, but her remarks may be applied to Chesterfield as well: "Enough my disputants. . . . Pray allow me to give a new turn to your debate; for I foresee, that if you grow warm on this branch of your argument, one of you will make him a saint and the other a fiend; though it is very evident to our cool apprehension, that he was neither, but . . . a very strange compound of both." This passage clearly reveals Hayley's power of discrimination. When read alongside most of the other contemporary memorabilia concerning Johnson and Chesterfield, the *Dialogues* is a persuasive document which must be judged favorably for its lively presentation of the two men.

ROBERT E. KELLEY

University of Iowa
Iowa City

TWO DIALOGUES;

CONTAINING

A COMPARATIVE VIEW

OF THE

LIVES, CHARACTERS, AND WRITINGS,

OF

PHILIP,

THE LATE EARL OF CHESTERFIELD,

AND

Dr. SAMUEL JOHNSON.

LONDON:

PRINTED FOR T. CADELL, IN THE STRAND.

M.DCC.LXXXVII.

ERRATUM.

Page 221, laſt line but one, for *ſeverity* read *ſerenity*.

ADVERTISEMENT

BY THE EDITOR.

As all necessary *Information*, concerning the *Scene*, the *Persons*, and the *Scope*, of this literary *Dialogue*, may be found in the following *Introductory Letter*—*I* have only to detain the *Reader*, while *I* tell him, that it was written by a young Cambridge Scholar, on a Visit at the House of a Noble Relation, to one of his Intimates at College.

Introductory Letter.

MY DEAR CHARLES,

ACCEPT, with your usual partiality and animating good-nature, the first-fruits of a petty but useful talent, which your kind suggestion first tempted me to acquire.

You may remember, that in those attic evenings of our college, when we happily escaped from less alluring society,

society, to devote ourselves together to Demosthenes or Cicero, you have often said, that an early facility in writing short-hand, would be a desirable acquisition for a young student, who confesses a very ambitious, but, I fear, a very vain desire, to emulate, in due time, those demi-gods of eloquence. Let me now inform you, that when you see me again, you will see a tolerable proficient in the art you commended. Whether my proficiency has been most quickened by my friendship for you,

or

or by my native ambition, I shall leave my dear Philosopher to decide, in one of those contemplative minutes, when a recent perusal of his favourite Plato has augmented his characteristic propensity to scrutinise human nature.

By the way, as the greatest of philosophers are a little apt to forget their own private transgressions, let me whisper to you, that you are an absolute traitor for reading Plato alone, especially as we had

agreed

agreed to read in concert the particular dialogues that our beloved Gray has honoured with his applause. Treachery, however, always includes its own punishment; and I have the ill-natured satisfaction of being convinced, that you have but half enjoyed what you have read in my absence. Perhaps, reading of every kind becomes more delightful and more improving, when we share the amusement with a congenial mind. As to dialogues, we have, you know,

know, determined the point, when, in reading thofe of Cicero together, we found, that his animated and graceful compofition received new fpirit from the pleafing interchange of two friendly voices. Perhaps you are not yet aware, that you are at this moment reading a fort of preface to fome new dialogues: fuch is the prefent that I have defired you to accept. I fee your furprize, and the perfuafion that follows it: — but in truth, my friend, you are miftaken. Had they

they been compositions of mine, I should not, by reminding you of Plato and of Tully, have imitated the simple dwarf, so happily alluded to by the lively Sterne;— in presenting my littleness to your view, I should not have presented to you the standard by which you might measure it. Nor do I send you the production of any writer, who, being less dwarfish than myself, and boldly endeavouring to emulate those literary giants, has attained, in some degree, that marvellous

vellous union of grace and vigour, to which they are indebted for their immortal reputation. —— What then do I send you? —— In truth, a rarity; and one, I trust, entirely to your taste. — I send you a faithful copy of real and spirited dialogues, that passed under the roof, though not in the presence, of a certain noble Lord, whose name is familiar to you, and where conversation, you know, is frequently said to assume a truly attic vivacity.—I do not tell you that the inclosed is perfectly

fectly in the ſtyle of your idol Plato:—it contains, indeed, no ſublime enthuſiaſm, nor logical ſubtlety on metaphyſical ſubjects; but you will find in it, what moſt modern readers would think, perhaps, more alluring, an ample and free diſcuſſion of all the merits and defects in two eminent and admirable, but very different writers, who, having lately cloſed their career, have left the ſurviving public at full liberty to ſcrutinize, to eſtimate, and enforce their reſpective claims to immortality.—

As

INTRODUCTORY LETTER. xiii

As these writers have been considered as rivals, you will find that the cause of each is pleaded with the affectionate zeal of an enlightened admirer.—As it generally happens in pleadings of every kind, each advocate is tempted, in praising his client, to indulge himself in some severe animadversions upon the opposite party.—Yet, for the credit of both sides, I am persuaded you will agree with me, that the whole debate is conducted with a liberal disdain of vulgar prejudice, and that all the speakers

speakers advance no more than what the particular turn of their own mind had induced them to confider as the dictates of truth and juftice.

By the rambling ftyle of their dialogue, you will perceive, that it was real converfation, and no formal compofition of fequeftered ftudy.— As you are fo fond of clofe reafoning, I mention this circumftance, to obviate your objection to paffages that, I am confident, you would otherwife confider as defects.—As to myfelf, self, being a less rigid votary to reason than my dear Philosopher, I am ever willing to sacrifice a few grains of logic, for an equal portion of spirit and freedom.

But it is high time for me to recollect, that, instead of hinting to you the value of my present (which might, indeed, be prudent, or at least very fashionable, if I were making a present to the public) I ought to tell you, as briefly as I can, the particular incidents that enabled me to send you this singular proof of my regard.

It happened, that in two days after my arrival here, my Lord was obliged to leave us, and depart alone, on some private business, for Ireland.—My kind and accomplished relation assumed the privilege, that she is used to take in the absence of her husband, and became (to use the title I give her, in my idle raillery) Lord Lieutenant of the Library — no trifling dominion, I can
assure

assure you, but of considerable extent, and admirably peopled with subjects of every class.—You will recollect the description I have given you, of the noble room my Lord has allotted to his books; and particularly the elegant and commodious little recesses in the apartment, that are excellently contrived to admit a multiplicity of volumes. Our little party consisted, for some time, of Lady Caroline*, an amiable and old fe-

* A fictitious christian name, substituted here, and in the Dialogues, for the real title of the speaker.—*Note by the Editor.*

male friend of hers, with her brother the Colonel, and your humble servant: for the young people of the house are still abroad on their travels.—After breakfasting in a chearful parlour, that commands a view of the grove, and the lake illuminated by the Sun as he rises, we have constantly moved together into the library. Here, as my passion for books is known, and indulged, I have sometimes loitered, in one of the recesses, and, peeping into various whimsical authors, have utterly forgot

got to join in the converfation; and fometimes, after giving the company a due caution not to talk treafon, I have endeavoured, while I was fcreened from their fight, to advance in my new crooked labour of writing fhort hand, by catching the difcourfe of the moment. One morning, when I had thus employed myfelf, I fhewed my manufcript to Lady Caroline, not indeed from the motive that influenced a certain philofophical fhort-hand writer, who, having a very talkative wife, took down, without

out the good woman's fufpecting his employment, all fhe faid in a week, and prefented to her a legible tranfcript of the whole; when, as my ftory goes, the honeft dame was fo fhocked by the horrid figure which her peevifh loquacity made on paper, that fhe rewarded the Philofopher, for his elaborate, tender, and filent reproof, by correcting her foible.—I was equally fortunate, though on a very different occafion. My fair coufin, whofe converfation, I muft fay, has as little to fear from fuch an artifice, as any perſon's can have, was amuſed with my work, and, as we happened to be alone when I produced it, ſhe thus imparted to me the project it ſuggeſted:—"You know, my dear Edmund, we expect our good neighbour the Archdeacon to paſs a few days here; you know what an idolater he is of Doctor Johnſon; and you know the Colonel's equal devotion to Lord Cheſterfield:—we will contrive to engage theſe two literary enthuſiaſts in an amicable debate on their reſpective idols. You

ſhall

shall invisibly catch their dialogue, as you have done this; and, to shew that we have acted with no insidious design, we will afterwards allow them the liberty of perusing, and, if either desires it, of burning the paper. —So said, so done.—I have only to detain you from the dialogue, while I tell you, that, as they are both men of a social and benevolent disposition, they were so far from being offended by this theft of their words, that each has had the good-nature to comply with my request, and not only revife, but correct and improve his portion of the debate. So that you receive their fpeeches, like the authentic printed orations of our eloquent fenators, corrected in the clofet, and ftill faithfully breathing all the warm fpirit with which they were fpoken.—I fhould add, that Lady Caroline fet a fort of little trap for the difputants, which caught them to our wifh:—fhe had placed on her own little table in the library, a quarto volume of Lord Chefterfield, with two of Johnfon's octavos

octavos upon it, and had left open one of the latter;—the device was succefsful, and very fpeedily gave birth to the Dialogue which is now before you.

TWO

TWO DIALOGUES, &c.

DIALOGUE I.

LADY CAROLINE.

PRAY, my good friend, let me afk you what tempted you to fmile in furveying the books on my table. I hope it implied no cenfure on my choice

THE ARCHDEACON.

By no means. To confefs the truth, Madam, I only fmiled (if I did fmile) becaufe because their position hit my fancy as an emblem of justice.

LADY CAROLINE.

Of justice!—how so?

THE ARCHDEACON.

It represented to my imagination the decisive triumph of the once indigent and neglected, but truly great Moralist, over the high-born and fashionable Wit, whose vain talents were, during his life, the idol of his country.

LADY CAROLINE.

Have a care, my good friend—believe me, *that* idolatry is not extinguished. Remember, my brother is close to you; and such an enthusiast, that if you begin

begin an attack upon his favourite, he will give no quarter to your's.

THE ARCHDEACON.

I would not offend the Colonel for the world: but I am sure, he has too sound a judgment, both in literature and morals, to consider these writers on a level.—He may perhaps be partial to the memory of Lord Chesterfield, from a personal acquaintance with that nobleman; and if so, I sincerely ask his pardon for having alluded to the public failings of his friend.

THE COLONEL.

Your courtesy, my dear Sir, is so engaging, and I have in truth such esteem for your judgment, that I could wish to think with you on all points. I am convinced,

convinced, indeed, that we agree perfectly in all effential articles, though our coats are fo different in their colour—and you, who have the happy art of uniting zeal and moderation in matters of higheft moment, will, I am fure, be candid enough not to think me either a fool or a libertine for admiring my Lord Chefterfield. As to my perfonal knowledge of him, I can only fay, it was juft fufficient for me to perceive, in a few accidental converfations, that the world were perfectly right in pronouncing him the politeft man of his time. But it is not on any familiarity that I can boaft of with this accomplifhed perfonage; it is on a deliberate furvey of his life and character, and a long intimacy with his truly attic compofitions, that I have founded my increafing creasing admiration of his talents and his merit.

LADY CAROLINE.

I told you our enthusiast would catch fire.

THE COLONEL.

Nay, my dear temperate sister, do not affect a prudish indifference towards an author you love. Severe as he sometimes is, and very provokingly so, on your sex, how often have you had the justice to join in my estimate of his excellence! How often have we lamented together, and with equal indignation, that hypocritical or senseless torrent of obloquy, which has been poured upon his ashes!

THE ARCHDEACON.

Confider, my dear Colonel, that the cenfure on your favourite, which you reprefent as unjuft, has not proceeded only from a few individuals, who might be eager to infult the memory of the eminent from the pride of ignorance, or the malice of envy. It may be regarded as the outcry of an offended nation. A whole people can hardly be inclined to pronounce fentence on any writer with malignity and ingratitude, efpecially on the dead. But there are certain unexpected offences in the moral world, which burft upon us with an afpect of fuch enormity, as feems to force from the lips of every unprejudiced fpectator, the moft rapid and

abfolute

DIALOGUE I.

absolute condemnation. There are some violations, I will not say of religion and of virtue, but of common sense and common decency, which an honest attention to the good of mankind forbids us to tolerate or forgive. I am afraid the sins of your favourite must be ranked in this unfortunate class. For my own part, I must confess I esteem it so dangerous a thing to pour the oil of licentious admonition on the blazing fire of youth, that I wish his Letters had been destroyed. And surely you, Colonel, who never exert the privilege often allowed to your profession, of treating serious things with levity, you, I think, can never wish to reconcile our minds to the horrid image of a father preaching adultery to his son.

DIALOGUE I.

THE COLONEL.

Good heavens! my dear Sir, is it possible that a man of your candor and discernment can join in the barbarous inference that has been drawn from the letter you allude to? If we are to be condemned so cruelly, on a few idle or wanton words, that escape in some luckless or unguarded moment, where is the mortal of sufficient purity to support this rigorous inquisition? not your great Moralist, believe me. If Chesterfield must fall by such a scrutiny, so indeed must Johnson. Most of those who have heard the common anecdotes of this justly-celebrated writer, have heard his reply to a person, who once asked him, what he reckoned the highest pleasures of human life? It is well known

DIALOGUE I.

that he named the two groffeft of our fenfual enjoyments, and without cooling the hot idea by one of his fix-footed circumlocutions. Shall I therefore call your great moralift a preacher of gluttony and incontinence? Truth and juftice forbid! yet furely I might do fo as fairly as you arraign my favourite, in confequence of a few fportive words in a private letter.—But let us not play the inquifitor with an aufterity that converts into a crime every cafual expreffion, and is pregnant itfelf with more evil than it profeffes to correct. Let us judge of books, and of men, not from a few fcattered failings in fentiment, ftyle, or conduct, but from the full and fair impreffion which a complete and deliberate furvey of their blended merits and defects may leave upon our mind.

If on this plain and ample ground, you are willing to enter into a friendly debate on the different portions of censure and of honour, that may be due both to Chesterfield and to Johnson, I shall by no means decline the contest; for, though I am most willing to allow that the latter will have much the more able advocate, I shall not despair of proving that my favourite (as you justly call him) was in truth, " take him for all in all," as good a man, as sound a moralist, and as eloquent a writer, as the renowned philosopher whom you particularly admire.

LADY CAROLINE.

I never heard a more tempting challenge, and I trust the Archdeacon has too much spirit to refuse it. As you are two

DIALOGUE I.

two men whom we may safely lead into a warm debate without the slightest fear of its consequence, I confess myself very desirous of seeing you engage. Though opposite in your opinion, and zealous in your nature, I am perfectly sure that your controversy can produce no painful or unfriendly sensations in the mind of either; and to me it will afford both pleasure and instruction—it will enable me to settle my own confused thoughts concerning two authors whom I am fond of reading, and who, to tell you the truth, both delight and disgust me to such a degree, that I shall be particularly glad to hear the good and evil in both deliberately examined and candidly compared.

THE ARCHDEACON.

They are Beings, my dear lady, that will not admit of a comparison.—Would you not be angry with me, if I compared my honest friend Lion, the noble mastiff who guards your magnificent mansion, with the sly and mischievous Fox that has lately invaded your poultry. Such a comparison only can be made between the generous Instructor whose lessons defend our virtue, and the pernicious Wit whose writings only tend to circumvent and destroy it.

THE COLONEL.

I admire the spirit and ingenuity of your simile; but, like a ball thrown with too much force, it rebounds so unluckily as to hurt yourself: for I must inform you,

DIALOGUE I. 13

you, that your honeſt friend Lion was almoſt condemned, a few days ago, to a violent death—and he might indeed have ſuffered with juſtice, not only for arrogating to himſelf much more than his due, but for mangling moſt ferociouſly an excellent little ſpaniel, who dared to lap out of their common diſh, and whom he ought to have regarded as a fellow-ſervant, of equal value with himſelf in the ſight of his bountiful and indulgent maſter.—After telling you this anecdote, I will not be ſo cruel as to add, that I think you have pitched on a perfect emblem of your great philoſopher. Yet allow me to ſay, that he certainly did not reſemble your old philoſophical acquaintance, the Demonax of Lucian (whoſe name has been improperly applied to him) in the want

either

14   DIALOGUE I.

either of faculty or difpofition " to play " the dog*."

THE ARCHDEACON.

I allow your raillery its full fcope. I am ready to confefs, there was a furly grandeur in the character of Johnfon. He was ufed to fpurn the effufions of vice and folly with a fervent and virtuous indignation, that was frequently miftaken for brutal ferocity. An inceffant zeal for moral excellence was his ruling paffion; and he had an un-

* " Peregrinus ufed to reproach him for laugh-
" ing too much, and being too familiar with
" people: Demonax, faid he, you do not act the
" dog well."—See the Demonax of Lucian, tranflated by Franklin, and infcribed to Dr. Johnfon; who is called, by the tranflator, the Demonax of the prefent age.

exampled

exampled power of extracting morality from every incident of life, from every appearance in nature. No man ever exerted more intense or more constant thought, to search into the essence of all goodness, on his own account, and to render his researches beneficial to mankind: it is on this ground that he is generally regarded as a teacher of true wisdom, inferior only to the sacred writers themselves; and it is for the interest of human nature, that we should guard the glory of such a man from the petty cavils of detraction, or the unintended injury of misconception.—For my own part, I should say, indeed, that I am more intimate with him as a moralist than as a critic. In the former light, I revere him as a second Socrates, far superior to the first: and surely you, Colonel,

16 DIALOGUE I.

Colonel, who, for a modern soldier, are singularly disposed to moral contemplation; you, the attentive father of well-educated children; you, I say, can hardly think of seriously comparing an author of this character to one whose compositions (if I may venture to use the vehement censure of my indignant critic) exhibit only " the morals of a " courtezan, and the manners of a dan- " cing-master."

LADY CAROLINE.

I thank you, my dear disputant, for blending politeness with your zeal. I perceive that your tender respect to female ears, has led you to soften one expression in the very bitter though concise invective you have quoted.

THE

THE COLONEL.

We are perfectly acquainted, you see, with the sarcastic gall of your great Moralist. But let me observe, that the keenest sarcasms, in general, rather prove the virulence, or at least the pride, of the accuser, than the vices of the accused. Indeed, your idol himself, to do him justice, instructs us how to value them, when he says, in this very volume, "Ob-
"servation daily shews, that much stress
"is not to be laid on hyperbolical ac-
"cusations and pointed sentences, which
"even he that utters them desires to
"be applauded rather than credited."
But let me read to you the close of this paragraph, it is admirable:—
"Few characters can bear the micro-
"scopic scrutiny of wit quickened by
"anger;

"anger; and perhaps the best advice to authors would be, that they should keep out of the way of one another." Here you find that your great Moralist, thought it hardly possible for an author to regard his brethren but with an evil eye; and justly, perhaps, we might exclaim, on this occasion,

His own example strengthens all his laws,
He is himself the microscope he draws.

Rarely indeed did he fail to magnify the defects of such as were placed before him; though his own great qualities were blended with such imperfections, that, if the latter were shewn to us through a glass, whose magnifying power was equal to his own, he would certainly appear as the most enormous monster

monster that ever rose into philosophical reputation with bitterness of language and brutality of manners. Indeed you may recollect, that in his life-time, his own virulence was often retorted upon him. He has been called, you know, "a respectable Hottentot," and the Caliban of literature. But alas! what is proved by sarcasms of this kind, on either side? Little more, I believe, than the lamentable prevalence of jealous and angry passions in the heated candidates for popular applause. For my own part, as I have, though I am no writer, a passionate regard for the real interest and glory of literature, I am grieved whenever I see authors of great genius condescend to hack and mangle one another, like servile gladiators, to gratify the rabble, instead of combating in a common cauſe, like free and generous citizens, againſt ignorance and envy, the peculiar enemies of their republic.

THE ARCHDEACON.

Here, my good friend, we perfectly agree—believe me, I lament, as ſincerely as you do, the jealous infirmity of exalted ſpirits, ſo very common among the profeſſors of every art, that many people conſider it as neceſſarily inherent in that fine texture of the human faculties which we denominate genius.—I am far from wiſhing to repreſent Johnſon as utterly exempt from a natural defect, which he had the rare magnanimity to own and the virtue to ſuppreſs; for what can redound more to the honour of any man, and eſpecially of a profeſſed philoſopher, than to have it juſtly ſaid of him,

him, that he assiduously regulated every improper movement of his heart by a powerful and majestic understanding?

THE COLONEL.

Rigid truth and justice, I believe, could never say so of Johnson; but, allowing you for a moment that they might, I can easily tell you what would be more honourable, or, I should rather say, what would render a philosopher a much more amiable being in my estimation; and it is simply this—to possess a heart so kindly fashioned by nature, that its own native benevolence should supply the place of your majestic regulator.

THE ARCHDEACON.

That is, you prefer a ready-made philosopher to one who has had the merit of making himself. In the quiet vale of private life, where no fort of competition awakens the turbulent affections of the mind, your undisciplined philosopher may be all-sufficient. But in a continual contest for popular applause, where the faculties are ever on the stretch, and where the passions frequently blaze in proportion to the activity of the intellectual powers; in such a scene, and such you know is the field of literature, we must not, I fear, expect the gentle voice of benevolence to be attended to as it ought. Authors, we know, are irritable to a proverb; and how rapidly they are hurried into wilful or blind injustice to each other, we see but too clearly from every period in the history of letters. But if such are the infirmities to which their condition exposes

poses them, ought we not to conceive a signal respect for that eminent writer, who constantly exerted his philosophy, and forgive me if I add his religion, to preserve him from these excesses? It is in this point of view, that the character of Johnson appears to me particularly noble. Where can we find an author, who, in running so long a career in the same thorny field, has done so much for the honour of his profession, and so little for the gratification of his private spleen? Insulted and reviled as he was perpetually, when did he write a vindication of himself, or a satire upon his enemies? It does him, I think, infinite credit, to reflect, that with powers particularly formed to make him the first satirist that ever existed, he chose to exert all the energy of his spirit in moral compositions

compositions of a very different nature; in such as might invigorate the understanding, without affording any food to the malignity of mankind. At the time when we may suppose his resentment to have been most awakened, when his character was acrimoniously delineated under the title of Pomposo, by a satirist of great celebrity, you may remember that he disdained to take any kind of revenge, and I do not indeed recollect, that he has mentioned the name of Churchill in any of his writings. His great mind was aware, that in some kinds of contention the very act of engaging is disgrace. He perfectly understood an important truth, which few indeed of his fraternity have had spirit enough to confide in, or temper sufficient to attend to, I mean, a maxim which he

expresses

expresses most happily himself in closing one of his admirable Ramblers, and, if my memory deceives me not, it runs thus: "Whatever be the motive to in-
"sult, it is always best to overlook it;
"for folly scarcely can deserve resent-
"ment, and malice is punished by neg-
"lect."

THE COLONEL.

An excellent maxim, I grant you, in many cases; and it reflects as much honour on the preacher, as a good sermon on humility would reflect on a certain prelate of our acquaintance, whose general demeanor might lead us to suppose, that he knew not even the name of that virtue. The forbearance of Johnson, according to your own account of it, was the offspring, not of charity but

of

of pride. He did not throw, indeed, upon paper, any deliberate invective againſt his opponents; but we learn, from the diligent retailers of his converſation, that his common diſcourſe was a continued ſtream of ſarcaſms againſt all who did not blindly acquieſce in his dogmatical deciſions; ſo that the commendation due to his pacific conduct, if rigidly examined, amounts only to this—he never drew out his heavy artillery againſt his enemies, becauſe he thought that he could demoliſh them with leſs trouble, and more ſecurity to himſelf, by the ſnap of a pocket piſtol.

LADY CAROLINE.

Come, come, my dear champions, this is but an idle, and, I think, an unfair

DIALOGUE I.

unfair fort of fkirmifh. I muft be the arbiter of your contefts, not only as to the iffue, but the mode of conducting it. Like the prefident at one of our ancient tournaments, I muft fee that the knights engage only in a generous and friendly conflict.—Let each be as zealous as he pleafes to maintain the honour of his own idol, but without reviling that of his antagonift. I profcribe, therefore, all bitter farcafms, as poifoned weapons, that ought to be banifhed from our lifts. To drop my metaphor, which, I confefs, I cannot very well fupport, let me remind you, that I expect a full and candid comparifon of the two illuftrious authors whom you refpectively admire.

THE ARCHDEACON.

My dear Lady, the very idea of such a comparison, is enough to make our lately departed Moralist feel a spasm of indignation in his grave.

THE COLONEL.

If we might literally interpret one of the many poets whom your Moralist has vilified, and exclaim with Gray,

E'en in our ashes live their wonted fires,

then, indeed, I should apprehend that the dust of Johnson might be disturbed, by our comparing him to a writer whom he seems to have hated with theological bitterness, and whose reputation he attempted to stab with the short, but envenomed

venomed dagger of a vindictive monk. But though I am far from thinking your favourite so virtuous and pure a character as you seem to do, I can readily believe that his soul is now happily purified from that leaven of sour infirmity, which debased, I must confess, in my estimation, his singular and exalted powers. I can believe, that if his ashes were indeed insulted by any indecent outrage (which Heaven forbid) his spirit now, like that of Pompey, described by Lucan,

Would smile at the vain malice of his foe,
And pity impotent mankind below.

Believe me, I am so far from being an enemy to his memory, that I think his writings and his life are both worthy
of

of being ftudied. In both, we may find much to admire and emulate, with much to cenfure and avoid. With both, I would only wifh to take fuch liberty as he feems to allow, where he tells us, that, " if we owe regard to the me-
" mory of the dead, there is yet more
" refpect to be paid to knowledge, to
" virtue, and to truth *."

LADY CAROLINE.

Very well, my dear, decent brother! After your paying fo ferious and juft a compliment to the grave of his revered Moralift, I think the Archdeacon cannot in courtefy decline your challenge, or imagine that the honour of his client may be wounded by a candid difcuffion of his caufe.

Rambler, N° 60.

THE ARCHDEACON.

Before I speak a word in reply to the Colonel, allow me to ask your Ladyship one whimsical question:—You know that we all love and revere you as a matronly model of female virtues. Conscious of such a character, should you not blush with indignation at the thought of being compared to the celebrated Ninon, or to any more accomplished courtezan, if any such can be found in the annals of gallantry?

LADY CAROLINE.

Your question is, indeed, rather whimsical; and, if I wished to evade it, perhaps I might justly say, in the language of our lawyers, it is not a case in point.—But, as I am eager to promote the

the friendly debate to which my brother has invited you, I will be very frank in my anfwer, and tell you my genuine feelings on your fanciful fuppofition. If the odd comparifon you fuggeſt was candidly made, and chiefly to ſhew what a different affemblage of virtues and failings may be found in different fituations (for all mortals, you know, have fome failings, and I am far from thinking thofe of Ninon the only blemiſhes that may be found in our fex); if, I fay, your odd comparifon was conducted with that extreme delicacy which it certainly requires, I believe ———

THE COLONEL.

Believe, indeed, my dear prude!— Come; if you are not confident enough to fpeak the true language of your heart,

heart, let me be its interpreter, and say, you are convinced that such a comparison would rather please than offend you.—There is a simple female secret, which every man, who has studied the fair sex with moderate assiduity and intelligence, must have discovered, and it is this:—The women who are most faithful in the practice of virtue, still delight in being told that they are equal in loveliness to the famously elegant daughters of frailty; and I question, if the cunning Ulysses himself could have flattered Penelope more agreeably, than by telling her she was as graceful as Helen.

LADY CAROLINE.

I am not surprized at this sentiment from an idolater of Chesterfield. But
I will

I will anfwer your maxim by another, which approaches, I believe, much nearer to truth:—The men who fancy themfelves moſt deeply ſkilled in the fcience of reading the female heart, are generally the greateſt ſtrangers to its moſt delicate fenfations.

THE ARCHDEACON.

Your Ladyſhip is certainly right; a true knowledge of the fineſt work in the creation, is not comprehended in the grofs or vain ideas of a libertine.

THE COLONEL.

I vehemently proteſt againſt your applying that title to my client; as I have engaged to prove him as perfect in his morals as your celebrated Sage.

LADY

LADY CAROLINE.

Be calm, then, my dear enthusiast; for what I want to hear is, a full, candid, and simple statement of the real merits and failings in the two celebrated persons we are canvassing: I wish to have a fair, comparative estimate of both, according to your own plan of considering them; first, in their general character, as men or citizens; secondly, as moralists, or periodical lecturers on life and manners; finally, as writers, regarding only their style.

THE ARCHDEACON.

Pray do not repress the Colonel's enthusiasm, because he is one of the very few men who may grow warm in a bad cause, without catching any infection from the depravity he defends: indeed, however paradoxical it may found, it is his own goodness that makes him the zealous advocate of vice; for the truth is, he has himself so generous and pure a heart, with such a quick delightful perception of elegance and wit, that he gives the possessor of these enchanting qualities, unbounded credit for virtues which were foreign to his nature.

THE COLONEL.

I ask your pardon, my dear flattering encomiast. I must not allow you, in thus holding out an unmerited and dazzling crown to your antagonist, to trip up his heels without beginning to wrestle. You mistake me entirely, if you

you suppose that I consider my Lord Chesterfield as a perfect character,

"*A faultless monster, which the world ne'er saw;*"

or as even possessed of that true greatness and purity which some of our English worthies have attained. I only say, that with splendid and most engaging talents, he had neither more nor worse vices than your exalted Philosopher, and that he is no less entitled to the kind remembrance of his country. This, I think, an impartial discussion of their lives and compositions may render as evident, as it is that they were both beings of the human species.

LADY CAROLINE.

However strong and sincere you may be in this opinion, I doubt a little your being able to persuade even our candid Archdeacon to agree with you; and, I believe, the good folks of the world, in general, who delight in that short and easy mode of proving their great love for goodness, which they find in idolizing a name for imaginary perfection; these good people would be shocked at your idea, and perhaps exclaim against you, as a horrid profligate, endeavouring to confound all the principles of right and wrong: but, as we give you full credit for motives directly opposite to these, I beg we may pursue this amusing disquisition. Some familiar words of Johnson, that I have just recollected,

recollected, suggest to me a plan for pursuing it, in the fairest and most satisfactory manner. You may remember, in the journal of his fellow-traveller, when he is displeased with Lord Hailes, " for publishing only such memorials " and letters as were unfavourable for " the Stuart family, he says, If a man " fairly warns you, I am to give all " the ill, do you find the good, he " may."—Do not you recollect this passage, my friend. I am sure my brother does; because, though I cannot repeat the whole sentence regularly, I know it ends with those remarkable words, " I would tell truth of the two " Georges, or of that scoundrel King " William:" words, I believe, that have had no little share in kindling the Colonel's animosity against your Philosopher.

pher.—But let us adopt the preceding maxim, of one giving all the good, and another finding the ill. Let the Archdeacon begin, by setting forth every thing that tends to exalt and throw a lustre on his favourite Moralist; my brother may add the dark touches, but without any sarcastic aggravation of the defects he may discover.—Then exchange your office; let the Divine freely display all the vices of Chesterfield, and the Soldier appear, I will not say his defender, but his apologist.

THE COLONEL,

Agreed!

THE ARCHDEACON.

Your Ladyship is undoubtedly very good, to assign me only that sort of task

in

in which my duty and inclination may go hand in hand; for, according to your inftructions, I have only to fhew the genuine dignity of the genius and virtue I admire, and to point out the real deformity of that diffolute elegance, which has made, I think, too favourable an impreffion on the fancy of my friend. Yet, honourable and pleafing as I muft own the office you have allotted me, I muft alfo confefs, what happens, I believe, very frequently to men furprized by unexpected honours, that I feel my mind dazzled and bewildered by the fplendor of my charge, and that I am diftreffed by no little fear of difappointing your expectation.—But let me reflect how I may beft fhew my obedience to the fpirit, though not the letter of your command. To enumerate all particulars

particulars that do honour to Johnson, is what I am ill-prepared to do, and what, indeed, could hardly be done in conversation; for it would be to give an extensive review of a long, laborious life, continually ennobled by new acquisitions of knowledge, or by new acts of goodness and magnanimity. I must content myself with only stating to you, as forcibly as I can, a few of the most striking considerations, that have conspired to impress me with peculiar veneration for this rare and exalted character. Let me remind you, then, that he was the son of a petty, provincial, necessitous bookseller; that, so far from having received any external advantages from nature, his figure was hideous, even in youth, to such a degree, that Pope, you know, was afraid he could

hardly

hardly be admitted as a preceptor into a noble family, from the horrid convulsive diftortions with which he was afflicted.—Good Heaven! when I confider from what humble and difadvantageous obfcurity he ftarted, and what pure eminence he attained, although penury, deformity, and difeafe were confpiring to impede his advancement, I not only perceive the marvellous merits of the man, but feel a fublime delight in contemplating the native powers of genius, and the genuine dignity of fcience, fupported only by virtue.

THE COLONEL.

Forgive me, if I remark a little miftake in your eftimate:—what you confider as impediments in his way, were fprings that pufhed him forward.—From his

his own account of his feelings, he muſt have had ſuch a conſtitutional indolence, that I queſtion if any motive, leſs cogent than poverty, would have induced him to ſupport the burthen of literary labour—except perhaps his ſecond ſpur of perſonal deformity, which, *" in a great Wit* (to uſe the words of " your old philoſophical acquaintance " my Lord Bacon) *is an advantage to* " *riſing* *."—But I aſk your pardon for interrupting you ſo ſoon, as I dare ſay you have many more obſervations to favour us with, that may fall within the firſt diviſion of our ſubject, as my ſiſter has chalked it out for us, and illuſtrate the character of Johnſon as a man.

* Bacon's Eſſay on Deformity.

DIALOGUE I.

THE ARCHDEACON.

Recollect, my dear Colonel, the beautiful verses that you repeated at breakfast with so much enthusiasm, and with perfect sympathy in the sentiment they express:

Ah! who can tell how hard it is to climb
The steep where fame's proud temple shines
  afar!
Ah! who can tell how many a soul sublime
Has felt the influence of malignant star,
And wag'd with fortune an eternal war;
Check'd by the scoff of pride, by envy's frown,
And poverty's unconquerable bar *!*

Thousands have had the aid of those springs which you consider as instru-

* Beattie's Minstrel.

mental

mental to the elevation of Johnson, but how few have risen, I will not say to equal, but even to similar distinction! Recollect, that from an obscure, necessitous, and unsightly being, he raised himself, not into pomp and opulence, for he had a noble contempt of both, but into that more enviable eminence of character, which enabled him to associate with the rich, the powerful, or the accomplished, and made him universally revered, as the great teacher of morality, to the most enlightened nation of the globe.—If we survey him in the period of his early difficulties and distresses, in that state, which has induced so many needy adventurers to act the part of a literary Thersites, and obtain a miserable stipend by ludicrous scurrility or declamatory malevolence, how

DIALOGUE I.

how different, how pure, and, I may say, how magnanimous was his employment? When his firſt proſpect of ſupporting himſelf as a poet was blaſted, by the failure of his Irene (a performance, I own, that could not ſucceed, for his genius was confeſſedly not dramatic) his high ſpirit diſdained to debaſe itſelf either by flattery or detraction, the two ordinary reſources of an indigent, diſappointed author. He ſought a refuge from the miſeries of want, in working on that uſeful, that ſtupendous monument of literary labour, his dictionary, or in producing thoſe periodical papers, which are juſtly regarded as maſterpieces of moral admonition.—Inſtead of finding him betrayed by penury into vicious or diſhonourable occupation, we find him not only labouring moſt laudably

dably for the real good of mankind, but leading a life as pure as those sublime lessons of morality which he bestowed upon the world.—We find him, though under the pressure of indigence, yet contriving to exert that virtue of noblest lustre, which most dignifies the opulent and the great; I allude to his charity, which was so perfect, so truly christian, that he was ready to share the little pittance he had with any brother in distress, more necessitous than himself.— Recollect, I beseech you, that marvellous effort of a great and a tender mind, the composition of his admirable Rasselas, in a few days and nights, for the purpose of relieving a sick and indigent mother.—Heavens! my dear Colonel, if such an act of literary heroism had been displayed among your admired Athenians,

Athenians, they would have raifed a ftatue to the author, in fome diftinguifhed part of their city, and have worfhipped him as an amiable demi-god, whom filial piety had exalted to the ftars.

LADY CAROLINE.

Well obferved, my good friend! you will certainly make a convert of me, for tears ftart into my eyes whenever I hear a great character celebrated for uncommon tendernefs or generofity to a parent; and I am wonderfully difpofed to admit, that fingle virtue as a fufficient proof of perfection.

THE COLONEL.

I have ever allowed, that there are feveral glorious points in the character of Johnfon: you have feized and difplayed

played them very forcibly.—I perfectly comprehend your pointed addrefs to me concerning our old friends the Athenians. You allude to my having faid, laſt night, that much as Johnſon had been celebrated for his intimate acquaintance with ancient literature, there is not a particle of true atticifm, or of Roman urbanity, in all his compoſitions. I really think ſo—but of that when we come to ſpeak of his writings. At preſent, I am to confine myſelf to his character as a man; and in that point of view, you muſt forgive me for ſaying, that however great his faculties and virtues may have been, they were evidently balanced by imperfections of equal magnitude and weight. As to your remark on the marvellous purity of your Moraliſt in domeſtic life, I will only make

this

DIALOGUE I.

this short reply :—If I thought it decent or fair to pursue such a scrutiny, I am convinced, by the report of his associates, that we should find his early days as much disgraced by actual licentiousness, as those of my noble client, whom you have called a libertine.—But woe to the man, who from wanton or malevolent curiosity, attempts to violate the sacred recesses of domestic privacy, for the mischievous satisfaction of exposing the secret or forgotten sins of the illustrious dead. Far be it from us, my friend,

" *To draw such frailties from their dread*
" *abode.*"

I will not therefore allow myself to speak of any but his most open and self-evident

evident imperfections. These indeed were so great, that whenever I review his character in my mind, he is one moment an object of my idolatry, and the next of my abhorrence. For, if I recollect what you have so justly commended, his noble readiness to relieve the distressed, I remember also, that he was an absolute Cain, who could not bear to behold the accepted sacrifice of a brother. Indeed he assassinated not a single Abel, but continually levelled his murderous sarcasms against the literary life of all his numerous brethren, the whole tribe of our contemporary authors. I believe it would be impossible to name one of this tribe, to whom he ever gave a full and fair portion of praise untainted by envy; and if we review his poetical Biography, we shall find

his

his detractive malevolence moſt conſpicuous in the lives of thoſe who lived and wrote in his own time.

THE ARCHDEACON.

I will not attempt to extenuate the baſeneſs of ſuch envy, by calling it univerſal—on the contrary, I am perſuaded it is by no means ſo common as we imagine; and we may thus account for the frequent imputation of this hateful quality, where it has not really exiſted:—All human works muſt have ſome imperfections, and in every art a profeſſional judge will ſee and feel theſe with peculiar quickneſs and force. He may fairly deſcribe them according to his feelings; yet, his deſcription being much ſtronger than the impreſſion which the object has made on leſs qualified judges, will to them, perhaps, appear as the suggestion of envy, though in truth it is no more than the natural result of intelligent and keen perception.

THE COLONEL.

Your reasoning is so ingeniously good-natured, that, for the honour of literature and the arts, I shall wish to find it generally true.—In the case of Johnson, however, I am so far from being able to admit it, that I am convinced, if we can on any occasions exculpate him from the charge of envious detraction, it must be on very opposite principles— not from the warmth and acuteness, but, to speak in his own phrase, the frigidity of his feelings. We know, indeed, that he was not fashioned by education, by habit, or by the original texture of his frame,

frame, to enjoy any nice difcernment of real delicacy, in life, in manners, or in compofition. In truth, it is hardly poffible that fuch difcernment could exift in a man whofe common behaviour was as coarfe as his paffions were turbulent, and who fhews us, in every point of view, that detractive malignity, and over-bearing arrogance, were his prevailing characteriftics.

THE ARCHDEACON.

Surely I may retort upon you, with more juftice, that it is not poffible for thefe odious qualities to have prevailed in a character, whofe name is held up to public veneration by fuch a little hoft of recording friends—in a man whofe talents and virtues afford fuch ample ground for panegyric, that his death

death has almoſt converted the whole circle of his acquaintance into biographers or memorialiſts.

THE COLONEL.

Well might the ghoſt of Johnſon exclaim, with poor Jaffier in the tragedy,

" *Hide me from my friends!*"

For it is indiſputably true, that his moral character has ſunk, in the good opinion of the world, in proportion as the memorials have appeared which were deſigned to do him honour. Indeed, it frequently happens, that an injudicious partizan does more miſchief to his idol, than the worſt of enemies. But, as the little flock of his biographers,

phers, though certainly not birds of the fame feather, are all amufing in their way, I am far from wifhing to ftrengthen my arguments in our debate by treating them with afperity. I fhall only fay, therefore, what, if the lady who leads the band were prefent to hear me, fhe would not, I truft, confider as any breach of that courteous refpect, which is furely due both to her fex, and to her talents:—I fhall only fay, that this little tribe of biographers ftrike my fancy as a group of bufy children, who having got a gilt fhilling, are very eager to exhibit it as a guinea, each rubbing it with an air of confidence, to encreafe its golden luftre, but fhewing, alas! at every rub, ftill more of that bafer metal, which they

they are all so solicitous to represent as gold.

THE ARCHDEACON.

Not so, my good friend.—Let us rather call them an honest, philosophical set of people, who, in analysing a magnificent mass of the richest metal, tell us truly the real weight of the pure ore, and fairly exhibit the little portion of natural dross which their experiments discovered.—But to quit our metaphor, and speak the plain language of truth and reason; Is not the incessant kindness, the lasting veneration, which Johnson has received from his most intimate associates, a full proof, in itself, that his excellencies as a man, and a companion, were infinitely superior to his failings? What more

DIALOGUE I.

more touching teſt of merit can we deſire for any character, than to find, that he was revered, even to idolatry, by his friends? Does not the high reputation of Socrates reſt ſolely on this foundation? He has been the idol of ſucceeding ages, becauſe he was juſtly idolized by thoſe faithful and accompliſhed recorders of his companionable perfections, Xenophon and Plato.

THE COLONEL.

Aſſuredly:—and as often as we review their affectionate accounts of him, particularly the very ſweet and ſimple portrait exhibited by the firſt, we ſympathize in the tender enthuſiaſm of the friendly memorialiſt. But what would the world have thought of the great

Pagan

Pagan Sage, if his fair and elegant friend Aspasia had left us a little book of philosophical anecdotes, in which we might read, that the great philosopher had rewarded her, for allowing him a noble apartment, and all the comforts of her magnificent house, by teazing, with argumentative and imperious petulance, her good, aged mother? What would the world have thought of him, if Xenophon had given us the narrative of an excursion, made to amuse his instructive master, by shewing him the bleak mountains of Thrace, and had told us, that when he presented him to his venerable old father, who dwelt in that country, the Sage, instead of entertaining his respectable host with colloquial wisdom, worried him so ferociously, that the luckless

DIALOGUE I. 61

luckless disciple must have wished for a muzzle, to secure his parent from the mouth of the outrageous brute, whom he had ventured to lead from Athens to a distant province, for the sake of shewing him as a consummate philosopher? Again, I may say, what would the world have thought of him, if the sublime Plato himself had represented his admirable instructor as the most selfish and disgusting glutton that ever appeared at a table?— Such are the points of view in which your favourite Moralist has been exhibited to us by his various biographical associates. Your excellent memory, my good friend, will readily suggest the passages to which I have alluded. I am far from suspecting all or any one of these writers of a treacherous intention to degrade their hero;—yet, what enemies could have contributed more to his degradation as a man, in the eyes of every candid and impartial reader?—I will not say it has happened by their fault; let us call it rather a fatality, for the accomplishment of literary justice—and it affords us an incentive to universal candour and benevolence, to contemplate the man, who had written the lives of many with a great portion of detractive malignity, destined to have memorials of himself so written, by a succession of his friends, that his character must sink in the public esteem, exactly as fast as their friendly records appear.

THE ARCHDEACON.

I cannot agree with you; for I cannot perceive, in my own mind, the effect that

that you suppose universal. I cannot perceive that I ought to esteem him the less as a man of virtue, because I am told it was his custom to eat in eager silence; though, I confess, it does not appear very consistent with the delicacy of friendship, to commemorate a peculiarity so disgusting.

THE COLONEL.

Well, my good friend, we will not argue this point. In favour of your great Moralist, I consent to strike the name of gluttony from the catalogue of vices. But allow me to ask you, if you could revere even the Pagan Socrates, as a philosopher, on finding him deficient in those primary constituents of a great moral character, justice and fortitude?

THE ARCHDEACON.

Moſt certainly not; and, let me add, that my veneration for Johnſon is partly founded on my idea of his having poſſeſſed thoſe noble qualities in a ſuperlative degree.

THE COLONEL.

To me he appears defective in both. Indeed we violate the name of Juſtice, when we ſuppoſe her to have dwelt in the ſpirit of a man who inceſſantly detracted from all eminent characters, and who hardly allowed any mortals to differ from him in opinion, without repreſenting them as worthleſs or inſignificant; yet Johnſon, for ſome time, contrived to ſupport a moral reputation as marvellouſly as Mithridates ſupported
his

his life. Your Philosopher, after fortifying his good name by many tumid sentences of morality, ventured on such envious gratifications as would have been immediate death to the credit of any other man; and the chemical king of Pontus, you know, as historians inform us, after breakfasting on antidotes ventured to dine safely on poison.

THE ARCHDEACON.

Take care, my lively friend, that you are not hurried yourself into the very injustice which you impute to my Philosopher. I allow you, that his strong and gloomy imagination very frequently discoloured his judgment. I lament the prejudices which led him to insult the poetic genius of Gray, and the genuine philanthropic heroism of our political saviour,

saviour, King William. Yet many allowances ought to be made for the prejudices of his early life, and that terrific ſtructure of his nerves, which gave ſo dark a tinge to his mind. As he courageouſly ſpoke his true ſentiments on all occaſions, it is ſurely evident, that he poſſeſſed the ſpirit of intentional juſtice, at leaſt, and of unqueſtionable fortitude. Where he was miſtaken, let us rather pity his errors, than emulate his acrimonious ſeverity.

THE COLONEL.

With all my heart, when I have once convinced you how very far he was from being that accompliſhed, practical Moraliſt, which you ſeem to have ſuppoſed, and how inferior, at leaſt in my eſtimation, to that calumniated nobleman, whom

whom with a proud baseness, peculiar to himself, he first complimented, and then insulted, without any real provocation. —Such was the justice of your great Moralist; who has indeed as little claim to critical mercy as any man can have; for he was himself a black hussar in the field of learning, who never gave quarter, or, I should rather say, he displayed his powers with a cold, phlegmatic, inquisitorial cruelty; and, as an ecclesiastical friend of ours said the other day, with an extempore paraphrase of the famous old verse in Ovid,

On their own rack, 'tis righteously decreed,
Bloody inquisitors themselves shall bleed.

THE ARCHDEACON.

Pray obferve, my honeft but too warm avenger of injuftice, how your accufation, by its own vehemence, defeats at leaft a part of itfelf. The force with which you defcribe the barbarity of Johnfon, furely tends to clear him of your fecond charge, the want of courage.—Indeed no charge can have lefs foundation. I queftion if there ever exifted a man who difplayed more invariably, in the character of an author, a more abfolute exemption from cowardice.

THE COLONEL.

So far from it, that you fhall find, he reprefents himfelf as a moft pitiful coward, and that too on one of thofe occafions

sions in which every man is allowed to assume the language of heroism. Every lover, let him be as unlike a hero as he may, is privileged by nature to tell his mistress, in a song, that he will banish her vexations, and protect her from all the world. But what says your brave author, in singing to his dulcinea? why truly this literary Cæsar of yours cries out, like a poor splenetic pretended Philosopher as he was,

Tir'd with vain joys, and false alarms,
With mental and corporeal strife;
Snatch me, my Stella, to thy arms,
And screen me from the ills of life.

Now put the stanza into prose, and his amorous entreaty is this—" I am " too great a coward to bear pain, either " in

" in mind or body: pray protect me, my
" good bolder girl, and hide me with
" your petticoats from the horrors of my
" exiſtence."

LADY CAROLINE.

Oh abominable!—Sir, this wicked brother of mine is laughing at us ſimple folks, for our ſerious attention to him. I am confident he does not give us his genuine ſentiments; for, three days ago, I heard him praiſe the eaſy natural tenderneſs of the very lines which he has now traveſtied ſo unfairly.

THE COLONEL.

Well, if you will not take my preſent remarks for ſound criticiſm, you muſt at leaſt allow that they equal in truth

truth and candour thofe critical obfervations which the great Moralift has made on Prior, Hammond, &c.—But to be very fincere with you; I perceive from this converfation, how very apt the mind is to take a ftrong bias in every controverfial career; for fince I began to compare Johnfon in my thoughts with one of my literary favourites, whofe memory I think greatly injured, all the imperfections of the gloomy Moralift have been fo multiplied and magnified, in my fancy, that he ftrikes me in this moment, not as one, but an affemblage of unamiable characters :—in religion, a flave to fuperftitious horror; in politics, a fervile bigot; in familiar fociety, an infufferable tyrant. I give you my real opinion as it rifes in my mind.

How far that opinion is the refult of delufive prejudice, or of a fair though rigid eftimate, you are certainly qualified to judge; becaufe I profefs to have no knowledge of the character we are difcuffing, except what I have derived from his printed works, and fuch memorials of him as are generally known. If I am wrong, I entreat you to correct me, for I wifh not to injure any being alive or dead; and, without retorting upon him the vile abufe which he beftowed on King William, I will copy his language fo far as to fay, I would tell truth of a fplenetic favage.

THE ARCHDEACON.

You are certainly too fevere, and for this reafon;—the foibles of Johnfon lying,

ing, if I may use such an expression, in the superficies of his character, disgust you to such a degree, that you do not allow yourself to search fairly into his deeper and more noble qualities.—But, as it happens in his language, when you have once digested his hard words, you feel yourself invigorated by the strong reason they contain; so with regard to the man, if you are once reconciled to the roughness of his manners, you will clearly perceive his many Christian virtues, for which indeed he might have obtained credit more readily, had they not been so rudely covered. Yet we cannot deny the merchant to be rich, who abounds in gold, because he keeps it in a bag of the coarsest texture.

THE COLONEL.

Your illustration is very ingenious, but not perfectly just. Though I agree with you as to the coarseness of the purse, I cannot allow your gold to be genuine.—To speak more seriously on a serious subject; I am aware that Johnson is held up to our veneration for the sanctity and soundness of his religious character; but surely, my dear reverend friend, it is an injury to the divine doctrine you profess, to consider this man as the model of a Christian. I can admit, with my whole heart, that he was a sincere believer in Christianity; but, to my apprehension, no real believer ever succeeded worse in seizing the true spirit of our indulgent and animating religion. His piety, great as it is called, was so far from being perfect, that it neither taught

taught him how to live nor how to die—
it neither infpired him with benevolent
gentlenefs towards his fellow-creatures,
nor with a chearful reliance on the be-
neficence of his God.

THE ARCHDEACON.

Without an oftentation of meeknefs
towards men, it taught him real humility towards his Maker. His piety
appears to you debafed by an excefs of
terror; but furely it argues not any
weaknefs or depravity of fpirit to tremble
before the throne of the Almighty.—If,
indeed, the gloomy caft of his devotion
could require any excufe, is it not fufficiently excufed by that morbid hereditary melancholy, which preyed upon
his mind, and rendered him, with all
his rare faculties, not lefs an object of
pity

pity than of admiration. This idea, instead of diminishing, increases my respect for his character—assuredly, it does him honour to reflect, that by long and profound meditation, he was himself the architect of his virtues, and that his imperfections were woven into the texture of his frame. His marvellous merits were all his own, and his blemishes the work of nature.

THE COLONEL.

At length, my good friend, we meet on such ground, as I have not the least inclination to dispute with you.—Believe me, I am as willing as you can be to consider the failings of Johnson as constitutional — all I contend for is this, that with so peccant a constitution, he may not be proposed to us as a model

del either of morality or religion.—The ancient philosophers, who maintain, you know, that virtue is not to be taught without the assistance of a proper natural disposition, would have not only denied his actual possession of consummate virtue, but the possibility of his acquiring it; since, instead of looking on the face of nature with true filial tenderness and gratitude, his gloomy spirit made him regard her only as a malicious step-mother, who exerted her ingenuity to embitter his existence. An affectionate delight in the visible creation, appears to me as necessary to perfect morals, as the spring is to the perfection of the year. How utterly destitute of that sentiment your great Moralist must have been, we may clearly perceive by his indignation against an

humble

humble and blamelefs woman, for pretending to be happy in fuch a world.— Yet, dark as this ftate of exiftence appeared to him, he could not practife even the wife precept of his pagan friend Juvenal, and (to quote his own fpirited verfe)

"*Count death kind nature's fignal of re-*
"*treat.*"

When I find him fo inferior in real purity and ftrength of mind to the pagan moralifts, I fhould think myfelf abfurd indeed, if I revered him as a model of Chriftian excellence, efpecially when I recollect, that with all his profound reverence to our blefled religion, he feldom opened his lips without finning againft the fpirit and the letter of the Gofpel,

Gospel, in calling a brother fool.—I am as ready as you are, my good friend, to ascribe both the gloominess and the asperity of his mind and manners to the vitiated organs of his very wonderful frame—indeed, the more I contemplate his character, the more I am convinced that the distemper which afflicted his body, if I may use a scriptural expression, entered into his soul. I am willing, therefore, to consider his defects rather as misfortunes than as crimes; although they appear to have operated against his happiness with the double force of calamity and of guilt. For, with uncommon powers to support either bodily or mental exercise—with all the advantages he derived from his successful labour, and the liberal kindness of his more intimate admirers—he seems to have been, through every period of life, a very miserable being; and no one, I believe, were it possible, would consent to purchase his rare faculties, by submitting to resemble him in every particular.—But whatever the sum of his imperfections may be, after that is substracted, there still remains such a portion of real merit, as will probably secure immortality to his name and writings. Believe me, I am so far from being an enemy to his fame, that I heartily wish the public would discover a more liberal disposition to pay him sepulchral honours. The subscription for his monument seems to languish, in a manner that reflects disgrace on this opulent and polished country. I wish, my good friend, that you and I knew how to quicken the munificence of the kingdom

dom on this occasion.—The nation that wishes to be ennobled by the production of future great characters, ought to be splendid in her memorials to departed genius.—I am amazed, that the zealous admirers of Johnson, have not been more eager to render him this tribute, since his title to such a distinction is admitted by those who had no personal attachment to the man, and who even think him, as I do, a strange compound of the most attractive and most disgusting qualities, that ever met in the formation of an author.—But I have said full enough and perhaps too much of his failings. Soldier, as I am, I assure you, it is more pleasant to me, on this occasion, to defend than to attack. Let me turn therefore from your respected Moralist, and hasten to the vindication of my injured favourite, the elegant, the witty, the accomplished Chesterfield.

LADY CAROLINE.

Not so fast, my dear hasty advocate. I cannot suffer either of my two disputants to evade any of the points that they have undertaken to debate. Pray recollect, that you are still to discuss the merits of Johnson as a writer.

THE ARCHDEACON.

Madam, the Colonel is a soldier of too much experience, to be very eager in attacking a fortress of any kind, that is secured by art and nature against every assailant. Let me be allowed to call the miscellaneous essays of Johnson, a heaven-defended city, whose palladium

dium is pure and perfect morality. As this can neither be overthrown nor pilfered by the boldness or ingenuity of any Diomed or Ulysses, the fabric, in which this eternal guardian is magnificently lodged, muſt be impregnable and immortal.

THE COLONEL.

Alas, my good friend! how many of such impregnable fortresses, in which not only morality, but religion herself, in all her purity, seemed to promise their preservation, have mouldered into duſt? It is possible, I fear, that your favourite, serious Ramblers, like many admirable sermons of paſt times, may, in a few centuries, be utterly forgotten.

THE ARCHDEACON.

Surely not; for although it is certain those excellent papers have all the serious purity of a sermon, yet they have also very different attractions. To me, the Ramblers exhibit a mental paradise, in which fancy and reason alternately entertain me with a succession of new delights, under the guidance and patronage of virtue and religion. While I read them, I feel (to use the words of their incomparable author) " my " heart rectified, my appetites coun- " teracted, and my passions repressed."

THE COLONEL.

I most readily admit, that the Ramblers, from the evident design of the writer, and from their intrinsic merit in many points of view, have very strong, and I sincerely hope they may prove successful claims to immortality. Yet, as lessons on life and manners, there are many productions of the same class, whose influence on my heart and mind is not only more pleasant, but more beneficial. To read the Rambler is, to my feelings, to walk through a stupendous Egyptian temple of black marble, furnished with some Colossal statues of ebony, and with here and there a little grotesque image, very lamely copied from ordinary life. I perceive, at every step, a strength and grandeur of conception in the dark fancy of the melancholy architect. I perceive, also, that in the course of his gloomy labour he had short fits of merriment, and that in those sportive moments,

moments, he was singularly awkward and ungraceful. In the whole structure, there is an air of awful majesty, that always fixes my attention, and frequently enchants me; yet, at the end of my circuit through its various apartments, I feel rather depressed and amazed, than animated and improved. Such is the effect which his most considerable work produces upon me; and that many others have surveyed it with similar feelings, we may conclude from what he tells us himself in the close of the last paper. The book is in your hand; give me leave to read the sentence:—
" Scarcely any man is so steadily se-
" rious as not to complain, that the
" severity of dictatorial instruction has
" been too seldom relieved, and that
" he is driven, by the sternness of the
" Rambler's

"Rambler's philosophy, to more chear-
"ful and airy companions."

THE ARCHDEACON.

I admire the magnanimity of this confession.

THE COLONEL.

You are very generous, my good friend, in allowing that quality to a poor discontented author, who tells us, in a fit of honest spleen, that he thought himself too wise for his readers.

THE ARCHDEACON.

It is surely true, that the serious air, and let me say the sublime beauties of that production, were the chief obstacles to its immediate success. Its merit was of too elevated a nature to be instantly understood by the frivolous multitude:—but it has at length been fairly appreciated by time; and the great moralist is now universally read, not only for the dignity of his sentiments, but for the force and lustre of his language. For my own part, I exult in the growing influence of his genius; I am happy in seeing it tend to the full discharge of that glorious office, for which every great mind should think itself fashioned by Heaven; I mean, the office of diffusing the light of knowledge and of virtue over millions of spirits inferior to itself.

THE COLONEL.

I will not be so ungrateful as to say, that I catch not any such rays from Johnson; but if I am frequently enlightened

lightened by his bursts of splendid sentiment, I am still more frequently darkened and depressed by his thick vollies of spleen. In all his writings, and in the Rambler particularly, he seems to me to bear a great resemblance to his own Suspirius, the Screech-owl, whom he represents, you know, " as settled " in an opinion, that the whole business " of life is to complain, and whose " every syllable was loaded with mis- " fortune."— He would, indeed, be the most meritorious of all moralists, if the merit of a preceptor consisted in trying to teach mankind that their existence is misery. I own myself devoted to more enlivening philosophy; for I could never find that wisdom and virtue are acquired by catching the contagion of constitutional melancholy,

or

or that the heart is made better, in proportion as the imagination is terrified.

THE ARCHDEACON.

Yet a man of your thoughtful turn, my dear Colonel, muſt ſurely allow, that in alluring men to pay a ſerious attention to their duty, a writer takes the firſt and moſt neceſſary ſtep towards making them better. It is not the gloom of melancholy, but the ſolemnity of religion, that gives ſuch a ſerious air to the compoſitions of Johnſon; and, inſtead of blaming the philoſopher, I think you ought rather to applaud the Chriſtian.

THE COLONEL.

I have already ſaid, that your Moraliſt appears to me to have miſtaken the true ſpirit

DIALOGUE I. 91

spirit of Christianity in his manners, and I think so no less in the tenor of his works, which, without mentioning those that are envious and unjust, have a general tendency to inspire a dreary gloominess of spirit. A soldier perhaps, my dear reverend friend, may have formed very erroneous notions of sacred things, which he cannot have studied sufficiently: but to my apprehension, the true spirit of our religion is more chearful than gloomy; for in what does Christianity surpass all the religions of the earth? not in its austerity, not in its terror, but in its benignity, in its comfort. It is chearful, because it excites us to the most attentive discharge of those tender and social duties which cannot be duly discharged without gentleness and joy. Other religions may
animate

animate the frame, by flattering some particular passion; as the Alcoran, for instance, undoubtedly flatters the two passions of desire and ambition. But Christianity, in my idea of it, accomplishes this end by the very opposite means: it melts down all the passions, and extracts from them the vivifying essence of universal charity.—Forgive me for thus throwing out the rough conceptions of a laical enthusiast, on so interesting a topic. I am sure you will forgive me, because I know we think alike, both on the importance and the benignity of our religion.

THE ARCHDEACON.

And let me remind you, my excellent friend, that our ideas agree also with those of the great Author, whom you are

too

too haſtily condemning. You ſeem to have utterly forgot, that the Rambler contains not only as ſublime, but as chearful a picture of Chriſtianity as the human faculties can exhibit; pray recollect the dream, in which a lovely figure exclaims—" My name is Reli-
" gion; I am the offspring of Truth
" and Love, and the parent of Benevo-
" lence, Hope, and Joy *."

THE COLONEL.

I perfectly recollect the allegory you mean, for I happened to read it

> It is remarkable, that the ſpeaker and his opponent ſeem equally unaware of a conſiderable miſtake in this quotation. The words indeed are in the Rambler; but in number 44, a paper ſupplied by a Lady, who, in copying the energy of Johnſon's language, has embelliſhed his work with the pureſt religious ſentiments.—*Note by the Editor.*

aloud,

aloud, the other day, to my fifter; and I remember, on our finifhing the paper, we both regretted that Religion, when fhe fettled herfelf in the mind of Johnfon, feemed to have excluded thefe her three children from her houfehold. To religious joy he appears to have been almoft a ftranger; he was not favoured with very long or very frequent vifits from religious hope; and that religious benevolence, which we frequently admire, as the immediate director of his pen, was continually overpowered and ftruck dumb by the ftronger voices of his more conftant companions, pride, envy, and fpleen. I allow you, that few authors have written with a more religious caft of mind than your Moralift; yet furely he difgufts his reader, not by being too much, but too little of a
                            Chriftian.

Chriftian. Religion has fometimes an effect fimilar to what is imputed to wine; inftead of giving new difpofitions to the mind, it ftrengthens and calls forth the humour it happens to meet, whether good or bad: thus the natural ferocity of Johnfon is feen to mount in a religious blaze, when, in his ramble among the facred ruins of Scotland, his imagination delights itfelf in conceiving that a ruinous fteeple may fall, to crufh the pofterity of the Scottifh Reformer. Surely, faid a friend of ours, when he firft faw that anecdote of Johnfon, this man wanted only the lot of being born in Spain, when the inquifition was eftablifhed, to have been diftinguifhed as the moft black-minded and bloody fupporter of that barbarous tribunal.

LADY

LADY CAROLINE.

Enough, my dear disputants, on this point. Pray allow me to give a new turn to your debate; for I foresee, that if you grow warm on this branch of your argument, one of you will make him a saint, and the other a fiend; though it is very evident to our cool apprehension, that he was neither, but, as most of you lordly creatures might be found, perhaps, in such mental dissection, a very strange compound of both.

THE COLONEL.

Very well, my dear Lady. So you think the sons of Eve, like the male heirs, who seize the whole estate in our modern families, have taken from their sisters

sisters all the ample inheritance of imperfection. Give me your hand, my poor sister! for if any son of Eve can be truly said to have done so, I am the man.

THE ARCHDEACON.

So you are, my friend, as far as the Lady is concerned: and let me add, that you resemble the modern heir in another particular; you have so contrived to get rid of this same ample inheritance, that we cannot even guess the amount of it.

LADY CAROLINE.

I thank you doubly, my good friend, for answering one compliment for me, and at the same time favouring me with another.—But come, we are idly rambling

rambling from our subject. You have still to consider Johnson both as a Poet and a Critic.

THE COLONEL.

In the first character he may be soon dispatched. We have only to say, what I think unquestionable, that he was inferior to the whole body of English poets whom he has so ferociously anatomized.

THE ARCHDEACON.

I ask your pardon. There is nothing finer in our language than his imitation of Juvenal, and his various prologues, particularly the very fine prologue that delineates the progress of the drama.

DIALOGUE I.

THE COLONEL.

Surely there is some degree of courtesy in allowing his name to stand on the list of poets, for having written the most frigid and uninteresting tragedy that can be selected from all the languages of the earth; and a forcible imitation of a declamatory Satirist. He thought himself indeed a great poet; and tried to bully the public into the same opinion, by the close of the arrogant prologue to his Irene:

" *In reason, nature, truth he dares to trust,*
" *Ye fops be silent, and ye wits be just.*"

This would have been bold language for any writer to have used, in speaking of his most fortunate production; but what is it, when applied to a performance which, instead of being inspired by his boasted patrons, Reason, Nature, and Truth, appeared to be rather the work of false, unfeeling art, and of pompous absurdity?—His critical bitterness may be partly ascribed to his great dramatic disappointment. Having utterly failed in his prime ambition to distinguish himself, and make his fortune as a poet, he conceived an eternal hatred to the whole tribe of poets; and, unluckily for that tribe, his powers of defaming poetical merit were as strong as his power to equal it was feeble. And hence, as I lately heard, a censurer of his criticism altered a title-page to his Lives of the Poets, and called them, " The " Lives of the triumphant Angels, " written by Lucifer the fallen." Indeed,

deed, he seems to have dipt his pen, not only in gall, but

" *In ever-burning sulphur unconsum'd.*"

In all his compositions, and even in his recorded conversation, when he is most virulent and ferocious, there is still such vigour of intellect in what he says, that, I must own, he hardly ever appears

Less than Arch-angel ruin'd.

THE ARCHDEACON.

I am glad you allow him some dignity as a writer, however diabolical.—But, my good friend, are you not aware of the extreme inconsistency in your description? You represent him as a most striking example both of feebleness and vigour.

vigour. In one point you muſt be miſtaken; for it is impoſſible that the ſame being can be both a giant and a dwarf.

THE COLONEL.

Pardon me!—that impoſſibility was realized in Johnſon. He was a giant in ſome faculties, and a dwarf in others.

THE ARCHDEACON.

Yet ſurely not a dwarf in that faculty, which is ſaid to conſtitute a poet—I mean, imagination.—One of his friends has told us, you know, and I think very truly, " His mind was ſo " full of imagery, that he might have " been perpetually a poet."

THE COLONEL.

We find he made the experiment, and could never be so completely.—His latest biographer, indeed, seems aware of his poetical and his critical failure, and appears to apologize for both, by supposing, that he is " to be " numbered among those poets, in whom " the powers of understanding, more " than those of the imagination, are " seen to exist."—But such a supposition affords us no very favourable or just estimate of the talents that really belonged to this wonderful being; for even the enemies of Johnson must allow, that a very vigorous, and a very quick imagination, was one of his most striking characteristics. The truth, I believe, is, however paradoxical it may sound, that a writer may possess the faculty

faculty of imagination in a high degree, and yet prove himself a miserable poet. Let any one try to read the Irene of Johnson, and he will be perfectly convinced of this truth. There are fine images, elevated sentiments, and splendid language; yet the performance produces only languor and disgust, because the author was utterly destitute of that sensibility, which alone can enable a writer to awaken interest and pathos. A poet, who has not the smallest degree of dominion over the passions, is as poor and impotent a being, as a king without subjects.

THE ARCHDEACON.

Such an author may fail in the drama, and yet excel in other branches of poetry.

THE

DIALOGUE I.

THE COLONEL.

I do not believe there is an inftance of any great poet upon record, who was unable, on every occafion, to affume the eafy air of nature, and to fpeak the language of the heart. Such inability, I think, attended Johnfon, both in verfe and profe. Yet, with all that deficiency, I feel he had faculties which juftly make him an object of admiration. He had a depth, an expanfion, a majefty of intellect;—he had an imagination that could prefent either grand or grotefque images to the mind, with infinite clearnefs and force; —he could lead or bewilder the judgment by ftrength of argument, or by logical fubtlety, he could amufe the fancy by fuch pageants as fhe is fond of
surveying:

surveying:—but I queſtion, if any poet or eſſayiſt ever exiſted, with leſs power of exciting either tears or laughter. With a total inability to catch or ſupport the proper tone of any aſſumed character, he appears to me, among writers, very like what a deformed giant would be in a company of players; who might, indeed, appear on the ſtage in the parts of Hamlet or Benedick, but would certainly not charm you with any dramatic illuſion, while you diſcovered, under his theatrical diſguiſe, the high-ſhouldered Goliah. An effect of this defective kind (to uſe the quibble of Polonius) ſtrikes me perpetually in Raſſelas. I hardly ever hear a ſentence uttered by the Princeſs, or the Lady Pekuah, but I ſee the enormous Johnſon in petticoats.

THE ARCHDEACON.

Had Raſſelas been the production of a Frenchman, his country would have called it a noble poem.—And ſurely, diſtinguiſhed as it is by livelineſs of deſcription, by dignity of ſentiment, by elevation and purity of language, we ought to eſteem it as the work of a poetical imagination.

THE COLONEL.

I have already declared my opinion, that the imagination of Johnſon was of the higheſt claſs. It was, indeed, a diamond; but, like the rarity that I lately read an account of in that excellent phyſician and philoſopher, Dr. Lewis, it was a black diamond, and malevolent melancholy was the *foulneſs of* of the jewel, to ufe the expreffion of the naturalift, on which *its black hue depended* *. You may tell me, that we ought to treat this melancholy with tendernefs, becaufe it was an hereditary misfortune; in that point of view, every perfon of common humanity muft be inclined to pardon and to pity its effects. But let not the quality, which was an infirmity in the man, be efteemed as a perfection in his works. His Raffelas, like the greater part of his other compofition, leaves a heavy and uncomfortable gloom upon the mind. You will tell me, perhaps, that the author wifhed to produce a very ferious effect, and that it conftitutes a part of

* See Lewis's Philofophical Commerce of Arts, p. 637.

his

his superlative moral merit, to have converted that idle or mischievous thing, called a romance, into a salutary book.—It may be so.—I can, indeed, conceive, that the old proverb concerning meat and poison, may be as true concerning books, our intellectual food, as it certainly is in regard to our ordinary diet. There may be minds to whom the pompous and dark fictions of your Moralist are both salutary and pleasant. To me, they are neither; for, instead of quickening my virtues, they only communicate their own gloominess to my spirits.—His imagination appears to me to resemble the Chinese bird, celebrated in that literary curiosity, " The Praise of Monkden, by " his poetical majesty of China." The bird is called Yuen. Its melancholy
cry,

cry, for it has no song, is said to awaken the whirlwind; and it flies only in the darkness of a tempestuous night.

THE ARCHDEACON.

Severely as you have treated Johnson, both as a poet and a novelist, there is yet one character in which you must allow him to stand superior to every antagonist. He was not, indeed, the greatest poet, or the most interesting novelist, that ever wrote; but, as a critic, he has no equal. His Lives of the Poets, though not free from little defects, and inclining, perhaps, to an excess of severity in a few articles, yet contain a mass of criticism, superior, perhaps, to all the united critical labours of the ancient and modern world. Different objections may be made to
different

DIALOGUE I.

different parts; but all voices conspire in celebrating the whole, as the rich production of the most profound and acute understanding, that was ever employed in the illustration of any single art.

THE COLONEL.

If barbarity can entitle a judge to preside over his brethren, you are undoubtedly right in considering Johnson as the prince of critics. His criticism has, to my apprehension, all the excellencies, and all the failings, of his other composition. It has all the powers that the head can give; it has none of the charms that the heart only can supply. If you examine his decisions on all our poets, you will find, that he ingeniously mingles as much malignity with his justice, as the nature of his office would allow him to exert.

THE ARCHDEACON.

This surely is a mistake. You are angry with him for his sarcastic severity to a few of your favourites, and therefore too hastily accuse him of malevolence and injustice towards the whole fraternity of poets—but, if his censure is now and then acrimonious, his praise in general is candid, generous, and magnificent.—The Lives, taken altogether, strike me as the most radiant crown of glory, that poetic genius ever received from critical admiration.

THE COLONEL.

I believe I can point out to you some very dark flaws in the brilliants you

you admire. But firſt anſwer me one queſtion; Shall you not think the malevolence, and I might add the abſurdity, of the critic ſufficiently proved, if, in his characters of many poets, I ſhew you paſſages where the cenſure is not only too vehement, but infinitely more applicable to his own writings, than to the poet whom he is cenſuring.

THE ARCHDEACON.

This, I confeſs, would abate my reverence for his judgment. But I am perſuaded, you would not find it poſſible to collect ſuch evidence as you deſcribe.

THE COLONEL.

As it happens, I have it ready to produce; for, being curious to convince

myſelf

myself how far his malignity to our poets extended, I amused myself, the other day, in selecting such passages as appeared to confirm my idea. Here they are—let me read them to you in order; and I think you will agree with me, that they exhibit rather a strong resemblance of Johnson himself, than a fair delineation of the unfavourable features in our great English bards.—I begin with a passage from his character of Shakespeare.

"In tragedy, his performance seems
"constantly to be worse, as his labour
"is more. Whenever he solicits his in-
"vention, or strains his faculties, the
"offspring of his throes is tumour,
"meanness, tediousness, and obscurity.
"In narration, he affects a dispropor-
"tionate

"tionate pomp of diction, and a weari-
"some train of circumlocution, and tells
"the incident imperfectly in many
"words, which might have been more
"plainly delivered in few.—Not that
"always, where the language is in-
"tricate, the thought is subtile; or the
"image always great, where the line
"is bulky: the equality of words to
"things is very often neglected; and
"trivial sentiments and vulgar ideas
"disappoint the attention, to which they
"are recommended by sonorous epi-
"thets and swelling figures.

"He no sooner begins to move, than
"he counteracts himself; and terror
"and pity, as they are rising in the mind,
"are checked and blasted by sudden
"frigidity *."

* Preface to Shakespeare.

Well, my good friend, is not all this a thousand times more applicable to Johnson himself, than to Shakespeare?

THE ARCHDEACON.

I must confess, it appears so; but in the Lives of the Poets, you can hardly have found any words so treacherously fitted to your purpose, or contrive to make them recoil so cruelly on their author.

THE COLONEL.

You shall hear:—and, that I may not tire you, I will omit many of the sentences in my list.—But what say you to the following?

"The compositions are such as
"might have been written for pen-
"nance by a hermit, or for hire by a
"philosophical

"philosophical rhymer, who had only heard of another sex*."—This indeed is partly true of Cowley's amorous poetry, yet it strikes me as more exactly descriptive of Johnson's various attempts to delineate female characters.

The malignity of your Critic towards Milton, fell rather on the man than the poet—and for this, you know, he has been very justly chastised. There is a sanctity in the poetical character of Milton, which secured it against any gross violation, from a person who piqued himself on his piety; yet in his account of this religious bard, your Moralist has contrived to insert a few malevolent remarks, infinitely more applicable to himself as an author, than to the sub-

* Life of Cowley.

lime and tender poet whom he detested.
—Let me read you my evidence.

"Milton never learned the art of doing little things with grace; he overlooked the milder excellence of suavity and softnefs; he was a lion that had no skill in dandling the kid.
"We read Milton for instruction; retire harrassed and overburthened, and look elsewhere for recreation."

How egregioufly false are these words, as said of the poet! how completely true when applied to Johnson himself!—The milder half of Milton's merit, this great critic had no feelings to perceive. He could juftly estimate the vigour of his imagination, but he could not difcover the tendernefs of his heart, which is exquifitely difplayed in the character

racter of Eve.—How perfectly has our divine poet caught the true tone of female nature, in those simple, beautiful, and pathetic lines, with which our lovely parent closes a speech in the 9th book!

*Adam shall share with me in bliss or woe;
So dear I love him, that with him all deaths
I could endure, without him live no life.*

How unfeeling must be the critic, who could represent the author of such verses, as utterly deficient *in suavity and softness!*

THE ARCHDEACON.

His hatred and injustice to Milton, which arose from his political sentiments, has, you know, been confessed and lamented by his friends.—As a counterpoise terpoife to this defect, let me remind you of the noble juftice which he has done to Dryden.—His account of this extraordinary poet, to whom Pope has fo juftly and fo pathetically applied the epithet *unhappy*, is executed, as the painters fay, *con amore,* and ftrikes me as the mafter-piece of our critical biographer.

THE COLONEL.

It is eafy to account for this pre-eminence; for in his whole lift of poets, there is no individual to whom the biographer bore fo great a refemblance, in the general caft of his mind, in his political, and, I believe, in his religious notions.—From fome of Dryden's failings, indeed, the critic was happily free, and to fome of his talents he has no pretenfion;

fion; but that they refembled each other not a little in their mental features, you will clearly difcover, by obferving how exactly the following paffages, from his forcible and juft character of Dryden, are defcriptive of himfelf.

"The power that predominated in "his intellectual operations, was rather "ftrong reafon than quick fenfibility. "Upon all occafions that were prefent-"ed, he ftudied rather than felt; and pro-"duced fentiments, not fuch as nature "enforces, but meditation fupplies. He "had fo little fenfibility of the power "of effufions purely natural, that he "did not efteem them in others. Sim-"plicity gave him no pleafure—he "could more eafily fill the ear with "fome fplendid novelty, than awaken
"thofe

"thofe ideas that flumber in the heart *".

THE ARCHDEACON.

Thefe paffages are indeed applicable to Johnfon, and fo doubtlefs are many fentences of praife, that we might difcover in his Biography: one honourable metaphor, at leaft, let us apply to him, out of the life from which you are quoting, and alluding to the clofe of his admirable eulogy on Dryden: "Let us fay of him, that he found the Englifh language a confufed heap of loofe ftones, and that he left them raifed by his fingle labour into a noble edifice, which amazes us by its magnificence, and delights us by its utility."

* Life of Dryden.

DIALOGUE I.

LADY CAROLINE.

I thank you, my good friend, for throwing in a little juft commendation to temper the Colonel's feverity.—He feems, I think, to be engaged in a cruel kind of a procefs; it is like the forcing a poor foldier to ftand before the mouth of his own great gun, and reluctantly blow himfelf to pieces.

THE COLONEL.

By no means. If an engineer, in levelling a cannon againft thofe whom he ought to have fpared, manages it fo ill as to hurt only himfelf by its recoil, the fault is doubly his own; and, however maimed he may be, he cannot be much entitled to compaffion.—Now I think Johnfon exactly in this predicament;

ment; and, when you hear the following extracts, I truft you will agree with me. For brevity's fake, I will confine myfelf to the lives of Prior, Hammond, Collins, and Gray, omitting feveral fentences in my collection.

To make you an immediate convert, my dear Lady, to the juftice of my procedure, I fhall begin with the character of your beloved Henry and Emma— " A dull and tedious dialogue, which " excites neither efteem for the man nor " tendernefs for the woman."—Every heart murmurs at the injuftice of thefe words, thus pointed againft Prior:—but obferve with what propriety we might write them, dropping only two particles, on the title-page of Irene, and call that Tragical Homily, " dull and te-
" dious dialogue, which excites neither
" efteem

"esteem for man nor tenderness for wo-
"man."

But hear the fuller estimate of Prior's talents.

" As laws operate in civil agency,
" not to the excitement of virtue, but
" the repression of wickedness, so judg-
" ment, in the operations of intellect,
" can hinder faults, but not produce
" excellence.—Whatever Prior obtains
" above mediocrity, seems the effort of
" struggle and of toil; he has many vi-
" gorous, but few happy lines; he has
" every thing by purchase, and nothing
" by gift; he had no nightly visitations
" of the Muse, no infusions of senti-
" ment or felicities of fancy.

" His expression has every mark of la-
" borious study; the line seldom seems
" to have been formed at once; the
 " words

"words did not come till they were called, and were then put by con- ftraint into their places, where they do their duty, but do it fullenly.—In his greater compofitions, there may be found more rigid ftatelinefs, than graceful dignity. His numbers are fuch as mere diligence may attain; they feldom offend the ear, and feldom footh it; they commonly want airi- nefs, lightnefs, and facility; what is fmooth is not foft. His verfes always roll, but they feldom flow *."

There's a curious portrait for you! If we knew not the painter, might we not fuppofe that it was rather drawn for the ftiff and pompous Johnfon himfelf, than for the eafy, elegant, and fportive Prior?

* Prior's life.

DIALOGUE I.

As to Hammond, Johnson seems to have criticised him with the utmost rancour, because he had been justly praised by Chesterfield; whom the splenetic savage seizes this opportunity to calumniate, by representing him as commending the Elegies of his departed friend, without having read them;—a charge not only absurd in itself, but inconsistent with the idea which this rancorous critic entertained of the noble editor's vanity; since the Earl is elegantly and justly complimented, in the very poems which he is supposed to have praised without knowing their contents.—I shall hope to convince you, in the course of our conference, that Chesterfield was as good a judge of nature, in poetry, as Johnson; and that he had the talent of representing it more faithfully, as an essayist,

than

than your great Moralist himself.—But let me now read the censure on Hammond.

"These Elegies have neither pas-
"sion, nature, nor manners."—Again,
"Hammond has few sentiments drawn
"from nature, and few images from
"modern life. He produces nothing
"but frigid pedantry*."

Do you not admire this charge of pedantry, against a poet remarkable for the easy elegance of his language, from another, who talks himself of *Arthritic Tyranny*, in an ode to the Spring?

But to shew you the difference between Hammond and Johnson, as poets,

* Life of Hammond.

let

let me read you these two short extracts from each.

What joy to hear the tempest howl in vain,
  And clasp a fearful mistress to my breast;
Or, lull'd to slumber by the beating rain,
  Secure and happy, sink at last to rest!

What joy to wind along the cool retreat,
  To stop and gaze on Delia as I go,
To mingle sweet discourse with kisses sweet,
  And teach my lovely scholar all I know!

Every man who has loved, must perceive, that in these verses, though I have injured them by placing them together, the passion of love is expressed with delicacy, spirit, and truth. Now hear how Johnson closes one of those curious compositions that he calls Odes.

K *Haste!*

DIALOGUE I.

Haste! press the clusters, fill the bowl;
  Apollo, shoot thy parting ray;
This gives the sunshine of the soul,
  This God of Health, and Verse, and Day.

Still, still the jocund strain shall flow,
  The pulse with vigorous rapture beat,
My Stella with new charms shall glow,
  And every bliss in wine shall meet *.

To say *Press the clusters*, is an odd mode of calling for wine.—But I quote the passage, to shew the tenderness of the poet to his Stella. Put the sentiment into plain prose, and it runs thus; —Come! let us get half drunk, my dear Stella, and I shall *then think you beautiful* and *myself happy*.

* Johnson's Autumn, an Ode.

LADY

LADY CAROLINE.

This is playing the barbarous critical tyrant, indeed! You out-Herod Herod!—But pray proceed to your extract from the Life of Collins, which I do not perfectly recollect. I only remember, that the critic mentions his personal intimacy with the poet; and I should therefore imagine, he must speak of his interesting compositions with an affectionate enthusiasm, sufficient to defeat your hostile purpose of turning the heavy fire of his critical battery against himself.

THE COLONEL.

Oh! your great Critic had too elevated and too stately a mind, to be touched by the partialities of friendship! Hear how

how he clofes a character of the poet, written when we might fuppofe his tendernefs to be quickened by the recent death of his friend.—" This idea which "he had formed of excellence, led him "to oriental fictions and allegorical "imagery; and perhaps, while he was "intent upon defcription, he did not "fufficiently cultivate fentiment. His "poems are the productions of a mind "not deficient in fire, nor unfurnifhed "with knowledge either of books or "life, but fomewhat obftructed in its "progrefs, by deviation in queft of "miftaken beauties *."—No one, I believe, can think the Critic fpoke too kindly of Collins in this early character;— yet, as if his judgment had been warp-

* Life of Collins.

ed by affection, in the subsequent life, which was not written, you know, till an interval of many years had allowed time enough for his *extreme* tenderness to evaporate, he added the following censure on the language of his poetical friend.—" His diction was often harsh,
" unskilfully laboured, and injudiciously
" selected. He affected the obsolete,
" when it was not worthy of revival;
" and he puts his words out of the com-
" mon order, seeming to think, with
" some later candidates for fame, that
" not to write prose, is certainly to write
" poetry. His lines commonly are of
" slow motion, clogged and impeded
" with clusters of consonants. As men
" are often esteemed, who cannot be
" loved; so the poetry of Collins may

" sometimes extort praise, when it gives
" little pleasure*."

Now, to my apprehension, every syllable, in both these Extracts, is infinitely more suited to Johnson, than to his injured friend; the greater part of whose poetry, as Langhorne has justly said of his ode on the death of Colonel Ross, *is replete with harmony, spirit, and pathos.*—But I hasten to the last article on my list—the insulted Gray. You are both of you so well acquainted with the Critic's extreme iniquity towards this enchanting bard, that I will only read a single short passage from those I have selected.

" The images are magnified by affec-
" tation; the language is laboured into
" harshness. The mind of the writer

* Life of Collins.

" seems

DIALOGUE I.

"seems to work with unnatural vio"lence, *double double toil and trouble.*
"He has a kind of strutting dignity;
"and is tall by walking on tiptoe. His
"art and his struggle are too visible;
"and there is too little appearance of
"ease or nature *.

Tell me, I beseech you, to whose writings may we most properly apply this exaggerated description? to those of Gray, or of Johnson? To me it appears to hit the tumid Rambler himself, so forcibly, that if any man were to attempt a small, but strong caricatura of Johnson as an author, I question if he could produce one with so striking a resemblance as this very paragraph exhibits.

* Life of Gray.

And now, my good friend, ingenuoufly fay, have I not convinced you, that Johnfon, in paffing fentence on our great poets, inftead of fairly reprefenting their petty failings, has frequently delineated his own heavier defects, and afcribed them to fpirits of a higher clafs, to whom they could not belong?

THE ARCHDEACON.

You have (I muft own) convinced me, that he was frequently unjuft; but I am ftill inclined to impute that injuftice, rather to the keennefs and ftrength, than to the malignity of his mind. I am perfuaded he always fpoke as he felt; but he felt blemifhes too forcibly, from the rigid integrity of his acute underftanding. Whenever he blames, I believe you may difcover
some

some little foundation for his censure; but he builds, perhaps, too large a structure on too trifling a basis. I cannot better explain to you my idea on this point, than by applying to him a lively couplet of Dr. Young:

His judgment just, his sentence over strong;
Because he's right, he's ever in the wrong.

THE COLONEL.

Very well! — if you acknowledge him to be in the wrong, I will allow you to estimate, as you please, the moral rectitude of his perceptions. My own idea of him, as a critic, is this:—His ill-nature, or, if you wish for a softer expression, his spleen, had, I think, a microscopic eye, which, whenever it happened to glance on a freckle

freckle in the face of any luckless muse, immediately made it a cancer.

THE ARCHDEACON.

If, as a critic, he was too severe, his severity may still produce a very useful effect on the trifling vagrants of Parnassus, by exciting them to think with more energy. And, let me add, he has one critical merit, which deserves the highest commendation; I mean, the merit of having rescued the dramatic muse from those oppressive and threefold fetters, *The Unities*.

The demolition of a perplexing poetical superstition, which had been sanctified by the reverence of ages, was the work of a noble understanding, very worthily employed, and a work that ought

ought to endear his name to every lover of the stage.

THE COLONEL.

I heartily join with you in this applause, though, in general, I have little veneration for your Philosopher in his critical capacity. It is Sir Henry Wotton, I think, who has called critics the brushers of noblemen's clothes; and, if his metaphor is just, we may say that Johnson, like a heavy-handed valet, has executed this office with such vehemence, as fretted to pieces the fine raiment of his masters.

THE ARCHDEACON.

Indeed, you are too severe!—But how great soever you may represent the mistakes of Johnson, in points that belong
solely

solely to taste and sentiment (on which, perhaps, we could hardly find any two minds in perfect unison) the great and solid portion of his merit must still remain entire. He strikes me like a venerable oak, which, though it may discover a few blighted leaves, and a little dead wood, perhaps, in the extremity of its branches, has a noble, sound trunk, of the most valuable texture. The world, surely, owes no little respect to a writer, who not only laboured for many years, with great sincerity and fervour, to improve their morals, but exerted his rare faculties for that purpose with such constant rectitude of mind, with such uncommon chastity of thought and expression, that I question if his numerous works contain a single word or allusion, which

the

the moſt modeſt female would bluſh to read in the preſence of a parent or a lover.

THE COLONEL.

Then you muſt think our fair preſident here a very ſqueamiſh lady, my good friend; for ſhe told us, you know, that ſhe was often difguſted both by Cheſterfield and Johnſon.

THE ARCHDEACON.

You are a very treacherous antagoniſt, in attempting to injure me ſo barbarouſly in the opinion of our judge. —But the equity of Lady Caroline is not to be corrupted or miſled. She will clearly perceive that you draw a very unwarrantable inference from what I advanced Indelicacy is not the only offence

offence in a writer by which a lady can be difgufted. As far as Lord Chefterfield is concerned, I can, indeed, believe that this offence was alluded to; for your dainty refiner of our manners abounds, I think, in fuch indelicate images, as are moſt likely to difguſt a mind fo pure as that in queſtion. But whenever Lady Caroline was difgufted by Johnfon, it was, I am convinced, by a defect very different from indelicacy, yet a defect of which fhe is equally qualified to judge—I mean, his critical injuſtice.

THE COLONEL.

She is not fufficiently honeſt, or, I fhould rather fay, fhe is too delicate herfelf to confefs, and demonſtrate to you, the contrary; but I will, on this occaſion,

DIALOGUE I.

occafion, be her interpreter. — There is, undoubtedly, a great degree of fuch purity as you have juftly praifed in the writings of Johnfon; yet, immaculate as you think him, I can fhew you a fentence in his biography, which is, perhaps, both the moft cruel and the moft indecent fentence that ever fell from the pen of a ferious writer; and I am perfuaded this very paffage was in my fifter's thoughts, when fhe made ufe of the word *difgufted*.

THE ARCHDEACON.

You have awakened my curiofity. Pray indulge me with an explanation of what you allude to, for I cannot even guefs at the paffage.

DIALOGUE I.

THE COLONEL.

Here it is, in the volume that lies open before us.—It relates to the unfortunate lady so pathetically lamented by Pope—you remember her history; I will only read the biographer's observation upon it.

"From this account, given with
" evident intention to raise the lady's
" character, it does not appear that
" she had any claim to praise, nor
" much to compassion. She seems to
" have been impatient, violent, and
" ungovernable: her uncle's power
" could not have lasted long; the
" hour of liberty and choice would
" have come in time. But her desires
" were too hot for delay; and she
                                    " liked

" liked self-murder better than fuf-
" penfe."

What fay you, my good friend, to the clofe of this paragraph?—I doubt if the pen of Aretine himfelf ever delineated the rage of incontinence with groffer or more difgufting energy.— There is a favage barbarity, to my feelings, in this paffage, that I want words to exprefs. It brings to my fancy the image of a cannibal, who, in finding the corfe of an unhappy, felf-flaughtered girl, inftead of breathing over it a natural figh of compaffion, tears the haplefs body to pieces, with a ferocious, farcaftic infult on the poor unfortunate being, who, in a fit of diftraction, had made herfelf his prey. Your great Moralift is the more inexcufable

excufable in this cafe, becaufe the unfortunate Lady, inftead of being fo outrageoufly eager to gratify her defires, appears, I think, to have been a tender penitent, not immured in a convent by the tyranny of a relation, but a voluntary recluse, who wifhed perhaps, but found herfelf unable, to atone for paft frailties by a long perfeverance in folitude and prayer.

THE ARCHDEACON.

The late accounts that we have all read of this unfortunate Lady, are very far from agreeing with your defcription.

THE COLONEL.

I know it; but I put no truft in the petty tales, which are fo confidently recorded

corded by the chroniclers of every idle hearsay. I cannot, indeed, perfectly vouch for the truth of my description, but I can shew you it has the colouring of probability. You may recollect, Pope himself tells us, in a note to his pathetic elegy, that the Lady was the same person to whom the Duke of Buckingham had addressed a copy of verses on her design of retiring into a monastery. I will endeavour to repeat to you a few lines of the Duke's poetry, and, luckily for his Grace's poetical credit, and my recollection, the lines I am trying to remember are the best in the poem.—O! I have just recovered enough for my argument.—The Duke describes a tender, enchanting mistress on the point of tearing herself from the arms of her happy lover, in a sudden gust of devotion, and proceeds thus;

"*And after all our vows, our sighs, our*
 "*tears,*
"*My banish'd sorrows and your conquer'd*
 "*fears,*
"*So many doubts so many dangers past,*
"*Visions of zeal must vanquish me at last.*"

Such are the grounds on which I represented this hapless fair as a distracted penitent, instead of an outrageous wanton; and if you consider the force of the passionate verses I have quoted, you will surely allow, that my conjecture is more specious, at least, than the improbable story, that she was in love with **Pope**. At all events, the Biographer has

has treated her barbarously.—I have heard, that he was intreated to cancel the paffage, while the proof fheets were before him, on account of its indecency and its injuftice; but that he perfifted in his favage refolve to ftigmatize the unfortunate Lady, that he might not lofe an opportunity of fhewing how truly he abhorred the crime of fuicide; to the verge of which, his own melancholy, I believe, had often conducted him.

THE ARCHDEACON.

I thank you heartily for this anecdote. I never heard any thing in my life, I never read any thing of this nervous this fublime author, that impreffed me with fo forcible fo grand an idea of his magnanimous morality! I now fee Johnfon in all his glory, determined to

exert

exert his rare faculties for the real good of his fellow-creatures, with a noble a divine indifference to their applause and their abuse!

THE COLONEL.

What! can you burst into a rapturous panegyric on his brutality?

THE ARCHDEACON.

Brutality! my good friend? Let us give a juster name to qualities that do honour to mankind. I grant you every thing you can wish, as to the severe and gross appearance of the passage you condemn. I will allow you, it is a sentence at which the cheek of a truly virtuous woman may turn crimson, not only from wounded modesty, but from an honest womanly indignation, in beholding so hideous

DIALOGUE I. 151

hideous a caricatura of female tenderness. But all these tremendous objections against it, tend only to encrease my reverence for the writer; and why? because I clearly perceive all the generous ideas that led him to write and to persevere in maintaining the passage. —Let us only examine the thoughts that must have passed in his mind on that occasion. He must have thought in this manner: "I have written a sentence, that is said to violate the elaborate purity of my moral compositions, a sentence over which envy and malevolence will exult, and at which decency herself may be disgusted;—but I know by what insidious steps the demon of melancholy may lead a poor idle girl, whose affections perhaps are wisely thwarted, to the

precipice

precipice of suicide.—If her piety will not save her, yet her pride may be rendered the instrument of her preservation.—I may resemble the ancient legislators, who, to stop the contagious passion for this crime among the women of their city, exposed the naked body of the self-murdered female. The sentence objected to, may check some unhappy woman on the verge of suicide, by shewing her how gross an interpretation the crime she meditates may receive.—Let the delicacy of millions be offended, if I can save but the life of one:—What are censure and applause to a writer, when put in the scale against such a possibility?—my heart tells me, they are dust in the balance."

So he reasoned, so he acted; and we ought

ought to revere the heroical benevolence and dignity of his decision.

THE COLONEL.

Nobly argued, my good friend!—I read in the countenance of the Lady, that in this article you have made converts of us both.——But I am astonished to find, by the progress of the sun, how our morning has slipt away—it grieves me to break up the conference, but I have some necessary letters to dispatch by the post of to-day.

LADY CAROLINE.

What! are you really going, brother? and do you mean to abandon the defence of your favourite Chesterfield?

THE ARCHDEACON.

Madam, the Colonel is aware, that on many occasions, and I believe in the present, a masterly retreat may be more honourable than a victory.

THE COLONEL.

"Do not say so—you shall not find it so."

LADY CAROLINE.

Well, then, let me make one request to you both—that we may not say a syllable more, either on Chesterfield or Johnson, till we are quietly settled again in this room to-morrow.

DIALOGUE I.

THE COLONEL.

I am much obliged to you for the idea; for in truth I should appear a miserable advocate for the accomplished Earl, whose memory I am to vindicate, if I had not a little time allowed me, to bring his cruelly mangled character to your compassionate contemplation.— This, I trust, I shall be able to do to-morrow.

Then will I speak right on—
I'll tell you that which you yourselves do know,
Shew you sweet Stanhope's wounds, poor poor dumb mouths!
And bid them speak for me: but were I Brutus,

And Brutus Antony, there were an Antony
Would ruffle up your spirits, and put a tongue
In every wound of Stanhope, that should move
The books around us here to rise and speak.

DIALOGUE II.

LADY CAROLINE.

WELL! my dear advocate for the noble delinquent, whom we are bringing to the bar, I may presume you are fully prepared to answer the heavy charges against him, since you seem to have got a collection of memorandums, as copious as a lawyer's brief.

THE COLONEL.

Pray do not discountenance, by your cruel raillery, a poor unpractised pleader, whose apparatus is only in proportion

tion to his want of talents and experience.

LADY CAROLINE.

I am glad to find that you enter with so much modesty on an office so daring as the defence of licentiousness; for the good Archdeacon and I have been in some fear, lest your quick imagination should inflame itself into a dangerous partiality to a character that your judgment cannot esteem.—He justly observes, that too warm an apology for vice, may imperceptibly injure an honest mind, by diminishing its due reverence for virtue; and he has just pointed out to me an excellent paragraph, in his favourite Rambler, which tells us how culpable they are, who have " used the
" light imparted from heaven, only to
" embellish

" embellish folly, and shed lustre upon
" crimes."

THE COLONEL.

You are good creatures, to be so kindly solicitous, for the preservation of that little rectitude of mind, which has fallen to my lot! But I trust your generous apprehension will subside, when you recollect the nature of the points that I have undertaken to maintain.—I have by no means engaged to exalt my Lord Chesterfield into a model of moral excellence; but I ventured to say yesterday, what I am now still more inclined, and I flatter myself more able to support—that, with splendid and engaging talents, he had neither more nor worse vices than your pompous Philosopher; and that he is equally entitled to the kind remembrance of his country. This, I think, is an innocent and juft affertion, that, to every unprejudiced mind, may be rendered as evident as it is, that to govern an unquiet kingdom, as a temporary viceroy, with dignity, and to be uncommonly clear in that great office, requires as much ability, and as much virtue, as are requifite to write a tumid moral effay, or to compile an elaborate treafury of words.

THE ARCHDEACON.

I might reply to your farcaftic mode of entering on this comparifon, by an allufion to the compliment paid to Titian, by the Emperor Charles the Vth: I might tell you, that the King can make many Lord Lieutenants, but not a fingle Johnfon.

THE COLONEL.

I believe the creative influence of regal power could much sooner make a Johnson than a Chesterfield. The command of a prince can, indeed, produce elaborate language, and ambitious morality; but genuine wit, and sportive urbanity, are so far from being *creatible* (if I may create a word) by the will of a monarch, that they very rarely condescend to appear in his presence. Perhaps they never appeared at court to so much advantage, as in the character of Chesterfield. I question if they were ever united to more political integrity; and how happily they may sometimes accomplish the irksome business of graver argument, we have a pleasant instance, in the anecdote of the noble Lord's

Lord's prevailing on the king to fill up a commiſſion with a name, which he had rejected with deteſtation. It was in 1747, when the Earl was Secretary of State. "I had rather have the Devil," ſaid the angry ſovereign, when preſſed to confirm the appointment in queſtion: "With all my heart," ſaid the lively ſecretary, who was waiting ready to fill up the inſtrument for the royal ſignature; "I only beg leave to remind your majeſty, that the commiſſion is indited to our right truſty and right well-beloved couſin." The king, you know, laughed, and complied with the wiſhes of his miniſter.

THE ARCHDEACON.

Your ſtory is a good example of pleaſantry well-timed. I will not ſay (what

I know many people think) that a few lucky ſtrokes of confident vivacity induced the world to deem much higher of his Lordſhip's wit than it really deſerved; but, giving him full credit, as a true proprietor of this graceful feather, I muſt not allow you to conſider it as equivalent to the more ſolid treaſures of Johnſon's moral wiſdom and virtue.

THE COLONEL.

Nor can I permit you, my dear and reſpected opponent, to aſſume as inconteſtible an opinion, which ſome honeſt people, indeed, have aſſumed too haſtily—that Johnſon was a compound of every thing that is morally good, and Cheſterfield of every thing that is morally evil.—If I can ſhew you,

you, that the accomplished Earl had in truth as much wisdom and virtue as the arrogant Philosopher, with his own rich inheritance of native wit into the bargain, you must certainly allow him to be the more admirable character of the two. That he was, indeed, neither less wise nor less virtuous than Johnson, is sufficiently evident to me, from a little survey that I have taken of what I may call the morning and the evening in the lives of each.—Let me set the two men before you, for an instant, in those striking periods of their existence. At the age of thirty, a season when the first whirlwind of the passions has subsided, and the mind of man begins to assume a settled temperature, how do we find Johnson employed? Why truly, in writing a rebellious pamphlet,

pamphlet, which his very biographer reprefents as mean in its execution, and deteftable in its defign.—Now let me direct your eyes to Chefterfield, at the fame age.—What was the noble Lord doing at thirty? In this year of his life, I find him giving an early example of that generous integrity, which he maintained through every ftage of his political career—and politely rejecting the advice of thofe, who recommended it to him to increafe the profits of a poft that he had juft accepted, by felling the fubordinate places in his difpofal. You may tell me, perhaps, that fuch an early comparifon of the two men, in a point of political purity, confidering the difference of their birth and ftation, is neither candid nor juft. Let us look then at the two veterans, when each

each was turned of seventy, when both were preparing to quit the stage of life, the Philosopher weary of having instructed the world, and the Wit of having enlivened it. At such a season, if the Philosopher had indeed been a man of sound wisdom and virtue, we might expect to find him calmly and chearfully looking forward to an immortal reward for the benefits which his labour had bestowed upon mankind; and if the gayer life of the Wit had in truth been a mere tissue of vice and folly, we might expect also to behold him, at this important season, sinking under the dread of a tremendous retribution. Now, are these the respective conditions in which we may actually contemplate these two opposite, but illustrious old men? No! it is just the reverse.

reverse. We see the imperious Philosopher looking back with remorse, looking forward with consternation, and strangely converting a justice of peace into a confessor, to tell him *more secret transgressions than he was willing to hear.* —Now take a view of the superannuated Wit, so unjustly suspected of a settled depravity in heart and spirit. We find him, and I beg you will observe the contrast, soothing the ills of departing life, and particularly that most depressive affliction, his long and incurable deafness, by pouring out all his manly and natural feelings, in letters of the most tender friendship to a venerable prelate—a prelate, who was long his bosom-friend; whom he had raised, in a generous manner, that did himself singular honour, to episcopal dignity; and who,

who, to his own credit, and to that of his noble patron, was diftinguifhed by the glorious appellation of the Good Bifhop.——It was thus that Johnfon and Chefterfield firft appeared on our clamorous theatre of the world, and it was thus they quitted it. They are now gone to their great audit, before the Judge of every heart, who alone, perhaps, can truly decide, which was indeed the man of moft wifdom and virtue. As far as their own books, and the printed accounts of both, can enable my limited faculties to form a juft eftimate of the two characters, I declare, and I entreat you not to condemn me too haftily for my declaration, that were I acting under Heaven as a judge, to decide the merits of the two, I fhould

I should rather give the palm of virtue to Chesterfield than to Johnson.

LADY CAROLINE.

Our good friend, I perceive, is amazed and shocked by the singularity and confidence of your opinion!—and even I, who know you better, must confess myself a little surprized at your carrying your partiality so far!—I thought you would have contented yourself with an *as wise* and *as good*, a kind of hand-in-hand comparison, as Shakespeare says: but your bestowing the palm of Goodness on a character universally condemned for immorality, is a stroke of whimsical enthusiasm that I did not expect!—Let me remind you, however, that we are departing from the plan we proposed to ourselves in this amicable debate.

debate. Pray recollect, that the Archdeacon is first to state all the flagrant and numerous defects in your too engaging favourite; and then you are to conclude, not with his apology, I find, but his panegyric.

THE ARCHDEACON.

As the Colonel discovers so much zeal in the cause, I beg that we may allow him to conduct the defence he has undertaken, in any mode that he chuses. You and I, my dear Lady, are at a time of life to be amused, instead of corrupted, by the magic of delusive eloquence, however subtle it may be; and for my own part, I am highly entertained in observing, with what acute ingenuity a very upright and religious mind, when under the
influence

influence of affectionate prejudice, can decorate a favourite, though faulty character. Our honest enthusiast has undoubtedly deceived himself, and he has, I am persuaded, sufficient talents to communicate that deception to others, during the moment when he is speaking. Yet, were he speaking to the world at large on this topic, I should be under no apprehension of his reversing the just decree of the public on the two characters in question; and for this short and simple reason—The public, however dazzled by my oratorical friend, would soon recollect the infallible test it possesses to decide the real merits of both; and wisely say to itself, By their works we may know them.—The Philosopher, however tainted by personal defects, has
bequeathed

bequeathed to us an invaluable legacy of the fublimeſt moral inſtruction; and the Wit, however decorated by perſonal dignities, has left us little more than an elegant manual of profligate advice, ſo improperly addreſſed by a parent to his child, that it has juſtly excited a general murmur of abhorrence.

THE COLONEL.

Surely, my good friend, you are ſpeaking only to try my temper. You cannot, I am confident, you cannot have ſeriouſly adopted the cruel abſurdity of the world, concerning the letters you allude to. O that I poſſeſſed indeed that divine talent of eloquence which your laughingly aſcribe to me, and for which I am ſo little faſhioned by nature or education! Were I really maſter of that

that enchanting power, I hardly know a subject on which I should more delight to employ it, than in doing juftice to a man who deferved fo highly of this nation, and whofe character has been fo bafely degraded.—We talk of the frequent cruelty and injuftice of Athens, to the virtue that defended her walls, and to the talents that immortalized her glory; but I queftion if ever any meritorious Athenian ever experienced fuch pofthumous ingratitude (if I may ufe fuch an expreffion) from his capricious fellow-citizens, as Chefterfield has received from us. Let me remind you, that he was juftly efteemed, for half a century, as one of the moft accomplifhed characters in this kingdom. He ferved his country as an ambaffador in Holland; and made the pureft characters of that republic

republic his friends. He served his country as a governor of Ireland, at a period of great difficulty and danger; and his virtues appeared to expand with his power. He served his country as a minister at home; and nobly quitted his place, the moment he found it inconsistent with his integrity and honour. He resigned, not to indulge himself in factious turbulence, but in literary retirement. Study and conversation were, indeed, among his favourite amusements, at every season of life; for the native cast of his character was rather gentle than vehement; and he opposed his enemies rather with gaiety than rancour. In the course of a busy and splendid life, he found time to write a few periodical lessons on life and manners, in which he equalled the first authors

thors in that branch of literature; and, having fufficiently proved his tafte, by his own admirable productions, he was univerfally regarded as the moft accomplifhed patron of letters. His manners, and his wit, were fo engaging, that he was long efteemed the chief ornament and delight of fociety, and the eminent characters of every country in Europe appeared ambitious of his acquaintance and regard. His latter days were embittered with many bodily infirmities, which he fupported, however, with a chearful and religious philofophy, in confidering this life as a fugitive dream, that he did not wifh to renew, and in thinking of his Creator, as he tells his bofom friend, the good Bifhop of Waterford, with more hope than fear.— So lived and fo died the Earl of Chefterfield,

field, respected by the world, and idolized by his friends.—But a Lady, who had great reason to think well of the noble Lord, seized the opportunity of his decease, to publish a collection of letters written for a very private and very particular purpose. She knew that they had been dictated by the parental tenderness of a good heart; and she did not foresee, that the public could ingeniously misinterpret them, so far as to call them the suggestions of an evil spirit; but, as there is a constant eagerness in mankind to seize, even the slightest opportunity of degrading an exalted name, as soon as these letters were published, an outcry was raised against them, by many hypocritical pretenders to goodness, and by many truly good people, who wanted either faculties or patience

patience to form a fair estimate of their author. Malevolent ridicule scattered her gibes on the father, so solicitously striving to improve the awkward person of his child; and mistaken piety represented him as a prodigy of wickedness, labouring to infuse all his own follies and vices into his offspring, and to establish a corrupt system of education, that would annihilate all the virtue of our country. But, after all, what is this master-piece of profligacy, when examined by truth and candour? It is a singular, and, in many points, the most admirable monument of paternal tenderness and anxiety, that the literature of any nation can exhibit; it is a work, that, instead of corrupting our sons, may rather stimulate their parents to a quicker sense of their duty, by shewing us, that a man, a man, in all the tumultuous bustle of busy, of gay, and of splendid life, could find time to labour with incessant attention in trying to counteract the peculiar personal imperfections of a dear, though awkward son.—O Chesterfield! I have read thee with the eyes of a father, anxious not only for the temporal but the eternal interest of his children; and my heart tells me, that in the sight of our great all seeing Parent, the work for which thou art vilified on earth must have more of merit than of sin.

THE ARCHDEACON.

Though every thing may be hoped from the mercy of the Supreme Judge, I cannot see how the common justice of mankind can absolve a parent, who even instigates his son to indulge himself in crimes

crimes that are eminently pernicious to the peace and happiness of the world.

THE COLONEL.

Is it candid, is it juſt, or, I ſhould rather ſay, is it not the height of iniquitous cruelty, to give ſo dark an interpretation to idle raillery, in a familiar letter, which, like the jeſts of private converſation, ſhould be conſidered only as the idle pleaſantry of the moment?—To defend licentiouſneſs, by ſaying, it was recommended only in a country whoſe cuſtoms appeared to give it a ſanction, is an argument, which, though it may extenuate the offence, is far from being, according to my ideas, the beſt vindication that we may urge for the noble Lord.—All the immoral advice of Cheſterfield, may be compared to a drug, which,

which, though it is rank poifon if fwallowed indifcriminately by the multitude, may operate as an innocent and ufeful medicine to a particular patient.— The difeafe of young Stanhope, to purfue the metaphor, was awkwardnefs in the extreme, and gallantry was the prefcription of Chefterfield. By giving his fon credit, in thefe private letters, for more influence over the fair than he was formed to attain, the father might mean no more, than to lead him frequently into fuch female fociety as had the beft chance of rendering him lefs an object of ridicule. Immorality of this kind, we hear every day in the fportive fallies of converfation between parents and children, where no real act of licentioufnefs is intended, and where no cenfure falls on the jefting preacher of very fimilar

lar doctrine.—It is particularly cruel, to give the darkest interpretation to the licentious levity of these motley letters, when the same correspondence affords us many serious passages of the purest morality.—There is a double injustice in the common censure on these admirable letters:—they are condemned as a general system, when they were expresly designed to correct the particular blemishes of an individual—they are condemned for not speaking more of morality and religion, when the author informs us, he had intentionally left those points to a worthy delegate. Yet that he touched upon them sometimes, and did it with all the affecting energy of a father truly anxious for the moral excellence of his son, I hope to convince you,

you, by reading the few following extracts.

Pray obferve, with what honeft and ferious warmth this fuppofed advocate for vice, exhorts his young difciple to the moft fcrupulous integrity.

" Your moral character muft be not
" only pure, but, like Cæfar's wife, un-
" fufpected. The leaft fpeck or ble-
" mifh upon it is fatal. Nothing de-
" grades and vilifies more; for it excites
" and unites deteftation and contempt.
" There are, however, wretches in the
" world profligate enough to explode
" all notions of moral good and evil;
" to maintain that they are merely local,
" and depend entirely upon the cuf-
" toms and fafhions of different coun-
" tries: nay, there are ftill, if poffible,
" more

DIALOGUE II. 183

"more unaccountable wretches; I mean,
"those who affect to preach and propa-
"gate such absurd and infamous no-
"tions without believing them them-
"selves. These are the devil's hypo-
"crites. Avoid, as much as possible, the
"company of such people; who reflect
"a degree of discredit and infamy upon
"all who converse with them. But, as
"you may sometimes by accident fall
"into such company, take great care,
"that no complaisance, no good-hu-
"mour, no warmth of festal mirth, ever
"make you seem even to acquiesce,
"much less to approve or applaud such
"infamous doctrines *."

Can the most rigid moralist, that ever existed, surpass the rectitude and the

* Chesterfield's Letters to his Son, Letter 180.

fervency of thefe admonitions—not delivered, indeed, with the bloated affectation of pompous and pointed fentences, but breathing the tendernefs and the warmth of a pure parental fpirit.

The Ladies, in their laudable zeal for the honour of their fex, are angry with Chefterfield, for reprefenting them as unable to keep a fecret; but they forget the great object he had in view: it was to form a minifter for foreign courts; and his caution therefore, on this article, was only guarding his fon againft thofe infinuating enemies, to which an Ambaffador is particularly expofed.

The noble Author is accufed of preferring *manners* to *morals*. I intreat you to hear how juftly he maintains, in the following paffage, the pre-eminence of the latter.

" Good

"Good manners are to particular so-
"cieties, what good morals are to society
"in general; their cement and their se-
"curity—and, as laws are enacted to en-
"force good morals, or at least to pre-
"vent the ill effects of bad ones, so
"there are certain rules of civility uni-
"versally implied and received to en-
"force good manners and punish bad
"ones: and indeed there seems to me
"to be less difference, both between the
"crimes and the punishments, than at
"first one would imagine. The im-
"moral man, who invades another man's
"property, is justly hanged for it; and
"the ill-bred man, who by his ill man-
"ners invades and disturbs the quiet
"and comforts of private life, is by
"common consent as justly banished
"society. Mutual complaisances, atten-

"tions, and sacrifices of little conveni-
"ences, are as natural an implied com-
"pact between civilized people, as pro-
"tection and obedience are between
"kings and subjects; whoever, in either
"case, violates that compact, justly for-
"feits all advantages arising from it.
"For my own part, I really think, that,
"*next* to the consciousness of doing *a*
"*good action*, that of doing a civil one
"is the most pleasing; and the epithet
"which I should covet the most, *next to*
"*that of Aristides*, would be that of
"well-bred *."

Again, in the close of the same letter,
"Be convinced, that good-breeding is,
"to all worldly qualifications, what cha-
"rity is to all Christian virtues."

Can any preceptor, my good friend,

* Letter 168.

exhibit

exhibit founder sentiments than these, either as to exterior accomplishment or internal perfection?

THE ARCHDEACON.

Like a skilful advocate, you have shewn us the fair side of your client; but had his book been entirely of this complexion, its purity had never been impeached. I believe, we might oppose to your quotations innumerable passages of an opposite tendency. But as, I must confess, I have not looked into this manual of politeness for several years, I shall not attempt to enforce my general charge against it, especially as you have answered that charge by a palliating argument, which, though it would hardly support any severe scrutiny, is, I am persuaded, so sufficiently conclusive to your

your partial good-nature, that I should despair of converting you.

LADY CAROLINE.

You seem perfectly aware of my brother's foible, which is, a generous propensity to think every writer virtuous, who displays the particular talents that afford him the highest pleasure. You might have found him, the other day, as warmly engaged in defending the moral character of Sterne.

THE COLONEL.

Pardon me! I only said, that if Sterne was in truth the sorry character which many austere people affect to call him, I supposed he was prompted to write by his good genius, that, in the register of the recording angel, the merits of the author

author might counterbalance all the sins of the man.

THE ARCHDEACON.

Yet, you know, that many human inquisitors have rather classed his writings in the catalogue of his transgressions.

THE COLONEL.

Yes! and I am perfectly aware that your splenetic Moralist was one of those inquisitors. But I can never subscribe to the severe sentence of a judge, when every fibre in my head and heart assure me of his iniquity.—There are glaring defects in the compositions of Sterne, but the general effect of them is meritorious in the highest degree. All the elaborate, all the ostentatiously moral volumes of Johnson can never impress on my mind such fervent sentiments of reverential gratitude to Heaven, or of good-will to earth, as I receive from a few pages of the incomparable Sterne. —Perhaps no author ever possessed, in so high a degree, the inestimable talent of putting the untuned spirit into harmony with itself, and with all around it. If I take him up in a restless or gloomy fit, he not only chaces from my mind every vestige of spleen, but leaves in its place a disposition to chearful piety and active benevolence.

LADY CAROLINE.

You have utterly forgot, my dear rambling enthusiast, the noble Lord, whose real or imaginary perfections you were to state to us; though I fancy, from the appearance of the paper in your hand,

hand, you have many more remarks to communicate for the illuſtration of his character.

THE COLONEL.

Thanks, ſweet remembrancer! Let me look at my references for a moment, and I will proceed in due order. We propoſed to compare Cheſterfield and Johnſon in three different lights; firſt, as men or citizens; ſecondly, as periodical lecturers on life and manners; and laſtly, as writers, in point of ſtyle.— Since I find the Archdeacon is too candid in his own ſentiments, or too indulgent to my opinion of the party I am defending, to dwell with great vehemence on the charge againſt my client, I ſhall conclude my deſultory pleading, by a few brief obſervations, arranged under the

the three heads I have mentioned, requesting my worthy friend to correct me where I am grosly mistaken; and I shall then entreat your Ladyship to favour us with your frank and genuine sentiments on the two characters in question.

I shall begin with pointing out to you a very striking difference between Chesterfield and Johnson, in an article which I consider as a great test of an amiable heart, I mean, Friendship. From the letters of the noble Lord to the Bishop of Waterford and Mr. Dayrolles, it is evident, that he took the most lively interest in all the concerns of those two valuable men.—Indebted as they both were to his patronage, and inferior to him in talents, he never speaks to them in a tone of superiority;

periority, but upon every occafion as a fincere and fympathetic friend. Pray obferve, from the following paffage in this correfpondence, how the fuppofed advocate for univerfal licentioufnefs in youth, fpeaks to thofe he loved on the education of their children.

"A father's care of his fon's morals
"and manners, is furely more ufeful
"than the critical knowledge of Homer
"and Virgil, fuppofing that it were,
"which it very feldom is, acquired at
"fchools: I do not, therefore, hefitate
"to advife you, to put your fon to
"the beft fchool, that is, the neareft to
"your ufual place of refidence, that
"you may fee and examine him often
"and ftrictly, and watch his progrefs,
"not only in learning, but in morals
"and manners, inftead of trufting to
"interefted

"interested accounts of distant school-
"masters *."

But my esteem for Chesterfield, in this point of view, is principally founded on his character of his bosom friend, my Lord Scarborough, one of the most beautiful and pathetic portraits of an amiable but unhappy mind, that was ever delineated by truth and tenderness; so very beautiful, that I think no one can read the composition, short as it is, without saying of its author, This man had indeed a heart for friendship, and the talent of describing those he loved in the genuine language of nature.

Now turn to Johnson.—In all his elaborate volumes, you discover no

* Twelfth Letter to the Bishop of Waterford.

vestiges

vestiges of his having enjoyed the inestimable blessing of true cordial friendship; no marks of that fond and amiable gratitude, which has induced so many great authors to delineate and immortalize the persons who contributed to their happiness or their glory. — It has been observed, that he never prefixed a dedication to any one of his various works; a circumstance that argues, to my apprehension, not so much an independent, as a proud, unfeeling, and surly spirit. For though dedications have too often consisted of base flattery to opulence and grandeur; they have frequently appeared as pleasing and graceful offerings to friendship, and sometimes as a proper tribute to particular stations. It is, I think, with equal malevolence and injustice, that Johnson accuses Addison of *servile absurdity*, in dedicating his Opera of Rosamond to the Dutchess of Marlborough, as the poet had exhibited, in a prophetic scene of his drama, the very mansion, of which the just liberality of the kingdom had made this Lady the mistress. His inscribing the Opera to her, was surely an act of blameless and becoming civility. This, indeed, is not the only instance of Johnson's malignity to Addison, an author whose life, whose writings, and whose death, exhibit such abundance of the purest merit, that I can hardly think the man a true and perfect lover of genius or virtue, who speaks of him in gross terms of sarcastic contempt.

But to return to the article that I was speaking of.—Had Johnson possessed a heart a heart for friendship, he must have enjoyed all the reciprocal delights and advantages of that blessing, in his long connexion with Garrick.—They had set out hand in hand, to make their way together through the chances of a world to which they were equally strangers, and had jointly borrowed five pounds, in a moment of mutual distress, on the credit of the future Comedian. Such a circumstance was almost sufficient in itself to have made them sincere friends for ever, had their souls been of the true friendly temper; as there seem to be few bonds of union more lasting among men, than that of having passed through early hardships together. In my own profession, I have seen the force of this cement among our soldiers very wonderfully exemplified.

fied. But there were other confiderations that might have made Johnson a cordial friend to Garrick. Their talents were of so different a nature, that no rivalship could exist between them; and accordingly we find Garrick, who was apt, indeed, to be alarmed at every shadow of a rival in his profession, was ever ready to bestow the most hearty applause on the real merits of his old associate. Patient under his dogmatical asperity, and indulgent to his humour, he almost revered and obeyed him as a parent; yet the splenetic savage, unsoftened by this filial homage, had the barbarity to mortify this bosom-friend of his early and indigent days, by excluding him from a little club, to which he sued for admission. This single anecdote of Johnson

Johnson is sufficient, in my opinion, to mark him for a brute.

THE ARCHDEACON.

You are running again, my good friend, into an excess of severity. You forget that Garrick had his failings as well as Johnson, perhaps greater failings, without an equal counterpoise of perfection. By talents of a class far inferior to those of the Philosopher, he had risen to the intoxicating joys of opulent splendor, and is said, you know, to have insulted, by an ostentatious display of his magnificence, his less fortunate old friend; who, like many other laborious men of letters, had been a drudge for years, without raising a competence for the decline of life. For my own part, I never think of these two extraordinary men, without lamenting in my heart, that they so little exerted the great powers which they both possessed, of contributing to the happiness and to the glory of each other. You know, my friend, that although I am in some points, as Lady Caroline calls me, an idolater of Johnson, I am far from adopting his gloomy ideas of human life. On the contrary, I think our earth, which is often a pleasant habitation as it is, would be for some years a delightful residence indeed, if every man seized the opportunity of doing the noble things within his faculties to accomplish, without indulging any malevolent or narrow-minded ideas.—For instance, had Garrick possessed a great soul, how happily might he have rescued his old friend from debasing himself in the eyes of many,

DIALOGUE II. 201

many, by the acceptance of that pension to which he had hastily annexed, in his dictionary, so odious a definition! How well might Garrick have spared, from his ample revenue, an annuity of equal value! and how much would it have added to his reputation and delight, if he had employed a part of that wealth, which he derived from the partial liberality of the public, in securing independence, not only to the friend of his youth, but to a mighty genius, who, from the peculiar infelicities that belong to authorship, could hardly earn more than his daily bread by such exertions of intellect as do honour to his country!

THE COLONEL.

Had Garrick possessed the princely spirit to confer such a benefit (which at times, I believe,

I believe, he really did) your splenetic Philosopher had too much pride to accept it;—though I perfectly agree with you, in thinking it more pleasant and more honourable to receive the blessing of independence from the bounty of a friend than from the pension of a sovereign, however gracious, to whose family and title the heart of the pensioner was known to have been a rebel.

LADY CAROLINE.

You amaze me, my dear disputants, by agreeing in a point where I differ so widely from you both, that I cannot refrain from an immediate declaration of my dissent.

Surely, to have accepted so large a gratuity from a subject, however exalted, must have been utterly inconsistent with

the

the dignity of Johnson. In receiving a pension from a sovereign, who has frequently shewn a disposition to correct the injustice of fortune towards literary genius, he had the sanction of custom and of propriety in his favour.

THE COLONEL.

As this is a point that depends chiefly on delicacy of feeling, you are probably in the right; though, I confess, I cannot agree with you.—But allow me to resume my argument. It is clear that Johnson did not love Garrick, though he had many reasons to do so; and it is equally clear, that the incurable envy of your moral Philosopher was the cause. I want no additional proof that he was utterly unfit for true lasting friendship. The friends of an envious man can have no security for the continuance of his regard, but their own infignificance. If they happen, by any fuccefsful talents, to improve their title to his affection, they will inevitably lofe it.—An attempt to maintain a friendfhip with an envious character, will probably produce a difappointment very fimilar to what was lately felt by a naturalift of my acquaintance, who, intending to preferve a favourite rarity in a bottle of pure fpirits, found it put by miftake into a veffel of *aqua fortis*, which annihilated the treafure that it was expected to preferve.

THE ARCHDEACON.

The force and aptitude of your fimile is a full vindication of my Philofopher; for, while I agree with you, that envy is, in truth, a corrofive of power fufficient to annihilate friendship, I must observe, that the long intimacy which Johnson enjoyed with many respectable and celebrated names, is a proof that if he was not perfectly exempt from this defect, its existence only added to the triumphs of his virtue.

THE COLONEL.

I cannot agree with you in your conclusion; for I find no public traces of his having praised the names you allude to, in the language of perfect affection; and surely those who have exhibited his character to the world, rather speak of him as a prodigy they admired, than as a friend they loved. He was, in truth, so great a prodigy, both in his faculties and his failings, that I hardly think it possible for any man to have contracted

tracted an intimacy with him much superior to the kind of friendship that subsists between a show-man and the lion that he exhibits. Indeed it has been observed, that the favourite and most adroit leader of the monster, who ventured to sport with him most familiarly, could not always withdraw himself from his paw without severe laceration.

THE ARCHDEACON.

The preference that your fancy gives to Chesterfield against Johnson, seems founded on your idea of your favourite's companionable attractions: yet surely, if the merits of the men might be fairly estimated by their powers of amusing a companion, the Earl could not triumph on this ground; for I apprehend his conversation,

conversation, if compared to that of Johnson, was like the soothing murmur of a rill, compared to the majestic roar of a torrent.—As to mirth, no witty repartee of the noble Lord, could more happily excite surprize and laughter, than the lively sallies of Johnson, both in prose and verse.

But your imagination is so much haunted by ideas of his ferocity, that you neither do justice to his wit, nor to the acknowledged tenderness of his heart,— which was so singularly humane, that I believe no author of his eminence ever afforded so much literary assistance to those who implored it. Persons who have been distinguished by the public display of any talent, are apt, in general, to entertain an important suspicious dread of debasing their dignity, by con-
descending

descending to employ themselves in any petty work for a benevolent purpose.— From this frequent and ridiculous foible the great humanity of Johnson completely exempted him. Whenever solicited by distress, he was ready, you know, to contribute either a prologue or a petition.

THE COLONEL.

Do not suppose me so blind, or so unjust, as not to perceive and revere his signal readiness to assist the wretched. He had, certainly, sincere and active compassion for great calamities; but this is a cast of mind very different from that which leads a man to perfect amity with the prosperous and the eminent. A poet, who is more kind than severe to

the

the character of your Philosopher, very truly and happily tells us,

He proudly splenetic, yet idly vain,
Accepted flattery and dealt disdain *

This disposition is indeed discernible in every portrait of Johnson; and surely nothing can be more incompatible with the true spirit of friendship. I conceive, therefore, that he entertained, for the persons who were most beloved by him, such a sort of regard as we may suppose the Man-mountain to have bestowed on those half-flattered and half-frightened Lilliputians, whom he deigned to elevate in the palm of his hand; and for whom he sometimes condescend-

* Poetical Review of Johnson by John Courtenay, Esq.

ed to soften the portentous sound of his voice.

But let me hasten to my second article, and compare your Philosopher with Chesterfield, as a periodical moralist.

As our religion informs us, that it is very difficult for a rich man to find the way to heaven; so may we conceive, that it is hardly less difficult for a man of quality, business, and fashion, to render himself equal to our accomplished authors. He who was nursed by vanity, and tutored by pomp, deserves, I think, no little praise, if he has delivered moral lectures not inferior to those of a philosopher, who had adversity to teach, and poverty to inspire him. In naming poverty, I cannot help reminding you of your Philosopher's very singular opinion, in regarding it as the only efficacious

cacious infpirer; an opinion which induces me to believe, that, had he been born in the rank of Chefterfield, he would have proved, if not the moft fenfual, at leaft the moft indolent of our modern voluptuaries. But, in the midft of many temptations to be idle and voluptuous, we find my noble favourite exerting his natural and acquired talents to improve the morals of his countrymen; and I will venture to affirm, that the moral papers contained in his mifcellaneous works, are full as well, if not better, calculated to anfwer their purpofe, than thofe pompous differtations of your Philofopher, where the two authors afford the faireft ground for a comparifon, in the fimilarity of their fubject. As a ftrong cafe in point, I beg you to compare, at your leifure, the admirable

mirable paper in Chesterfield, on the luxury of the table (which forms the sixteenth number of a periodical work, intitled Common Sense) with the paper on gluttony in your favourite Rambler.—If you compare also the introductory number in each of these publications, you will clearly perceive, I think, that the talents of Chesterfield were more suited, than those of Johnson, to the production of attractive and useful little lectures on life and manners. If you want farther proofs of this assertion, you may find them, I am persuaded, in the papers that he contributed to *The World*, particularly those on drinking, and civility, which live in the memory of every reader.—As Moralists, they seem to bear the same relation to each other that exists between the elegant,

DIALOGUE II.

gant, the penetrating Horace, and the forcible declamatory Juvenal. The engaging eafe of Chefterfield's ftyle, and the fportive graces of his wit, were peculiarly adapted to render him excellent as the effayift of a day. When they are compared together in this light, Johnfon is to Chefterfield what the Piony is to the Rofe—of a grander form, of more forcible and richer colouring, yet not fo pleafant; to be furveyed with diftant admiration, but not eagerly received into the bofom.

THE ARCHDEACON.

I will not be fo barbarous to your flowery metaphor, as to fay, that I prefume you mean only the Canker-rofe.

LADY CAROLINE.

Very well, my good friend!—this is a fair and very gentle touch of retaliation for all the severity with which your admired Philosopher has been treated. I confess, I have expected you to retaliate with much greater warmth on the weak side of your antagonist—I mean, the irreligion of his favourite.

THE ARCHDEACON.

To speak honestly, I could not in my conscience attack my adversary on that ground; for I perfectly recollect that Lord Chesterfield repeatedly inculcates, not only the most decent respect to religion herself, but to all her ministers. I am afraid, indeed, that his religious sentiments were not such as I, who am

by

by no means one of his profest admirers, most sincerely wish them to have been; yet, as this is a business between his own heart and Heaven, I do not conceive that any man has a right to suppose him an infidel, and then to censure him on the supposition.—This would be contrary to the fundamental principles of English liberty and justice, not to speak of it as a violation of Christian charity.

THE COLONEL.

I reverence you, my worthy friend, for this candour, and wish it were universal.—Chesterfield is condemned as irreligious; yet, so far from finding any traces of this offence in his writings, I find, that in one of his French letters he expresly condemns the irreligion of Voltaire,

Voltaire, partial as he was to that enchanting writer, from a perſonal acquaintance.—Cheſterfield is alſo condemned as a Frenchified fop; yet no man has written more forcibly againſt our copying the follies of France. Indeed, no man ſeems to have better underſtood or more highly valued the liberties of his country; and with what ſpirit he could ſupport the manly frankneſs and undaunted truth of the Engliſh character, in ſpeaking to a Frenchman, we have a ſtriking example in his letter to the Abbé de la Ville, the French miniſter at the Hague, on ſeveral particulars relating to the battle of Fontenoy. He has indeed been cruelly depreciated. Your Philoſopher, you know, very mercifully conſidered him as a *rotten poſt*, to uſe his own gentle phraſe; but

but if there were some unsound parts
(and who is perfect?) in the character of
the noble Lord, there was, I apprehend,
a still larger portion of touchwood in
the Philosopher himself.—I have never
seen the letter in which he renounced
the patronage, that he appeared to have
contemplated with no little satisfaction,
but, from all the accounts that I have
met with of that incident, I think we
may rather blame the splenetic pride of
Johnson, than the insolence or meanness of Chesterfield.—In the sarcasms
which they levelled at each other, the
latter surely approaches nearest to the
truth: the Critic was unquestionably
more like a savage than the Wit was like
a dancing-master.—Chesterfield had his
foibles and his vices. He was, in his
early life, a slave to the tyrannous vice

of

of gaming; but how ingenuously and parentally does he confess and lament it in his letters!—and, give me leave to add, that he once derived no little honour from a signal victory over this despotic passion. I allude to his conduct as Lord Lieutenant of Ireland.—You know that he banished gaming entirely from the castle of Dublin; and surely the man is entitled to credit for some nobleness of mind, who enters on the exercise of sovereign power by the sacrifice of his own darling defect.—Believe me, I am not blind to his private failings, and I heartily wish, for his own happiness, that they had never existed; but I still assert, that he had public merit sufficient to balance all his imperfections. Let hypocrisy and malevolence, or, if you please, let virtue herself deride him to the uttermost,

termoſt, as a vain and licentious puppet of quality—I ſhall never ceaſe to think, that he has many genuine claims to that laſting glory which he had the ſpirit to love and to purſue: nor is he leſs entitled to the grateful remembrance of our country, than the arrogant and ſplenetic dogmatiſt, who has vilified the heroiſm of our Kings, and the genius of our Bards; a writer of verſes, not from the impulſe of nature, but the ſuggeſtions of intereſt or ſpleen; a critic, not from an enthuſiaſtic delight in poetry, but an envious hatred to poets.

THE ARCHDEACON.

That is a point which Time will ſettle with his uſual unfailing juſtice.—Though mankind are not always happy enough to diſtinguiſh their real friends from their

their foes, yet their judgment is generally juft, when the candidate for their applaufe has nothing to truft to but the pofthumous influence of his works. —Whatever charity may hope concerning the fuppofed irreligion of Chefterfield, his immorality has too glaring an appearance to admit any doubt of its exiftence; and the man who is vain and profligate enough to boaft of his vices, is, I muft confefs, in my opinion, very far from deferving fuch an advocate as your favourite has found. Indeed the more rigid friends of virtue and religion may almoft blufh with indignation, in feeing two characters fo very different compared to each other.—Johnfon, the refuge and the friend of every being in diftrefs, compared to the oftentatious man of quality, who affected to be the patron of talents,

talents, which he wanted erudition to estimate, and liberality to reward—Johnson, the eternal Moralist, who made every social amusement a step in the acquisition of knowledge, or in the improvement of the heart, compared to the licentious Wit, whose only ambition was to dazzle and amuse—Johnson, to hasten at once to that aweful scene where the comparison is not only most obvious but most important—Johnson closing a life of virtue and religion with faith in his Redeemer, and with humility sufficient to tremble with aweful doubts of his own exemplary merit, compared to Chesterfield, finishing a frivolous and dissolute existence with the affected severity of a pagan Philosopher.

DIALOGUE II.

THE COLONEL.

If either party could have reason to blush indignantly at the comparison, I maintain it must be Chesterfield—Chesterfield, the enchanting companion, whose conversation was a model of the most enlivening politeness, compared to the surly dogmatist, whose habitual discourse was a compound of arrogance and spleen—Chesterfield, the accomplished, the diligent ambassador, who never lost a morning hour, compared to the lazy Moralist, who tells us, he wasted half his life in resolving to rise early, and in breaking that resolve—Chesterfield, the friendly editor, the just and delicate panegyrist of one elegant and tender poet, compared to the invidious biographer, who has scattered

his

his inexhauftible gall over the whole choir of Britifh bards—Chefterfield, the patriotic fenator, pleading with elegance and energy for the freedom of the ftage, compared to the fervile author, induced by his political bigotry to write againft the liberty of the prefs — Chefterfield, the beneficent viceroy, who governed Ireland in fuch a manner as to merit and receive the praife and benedictions of that lively people, compared to the moody traveller who vifited Scotland to infult its nakednefs, and to pour his fuperftitious execrations on the innocent defcendants of its too zealous reformer —Chefterfield, in fhort, to finifh with that important fcene in which all men, however different in character and condition, muft inevitably afford room for the moft ftriking comparifon—Chefter-field,

field, I say, the real Sage, ready and willing to die, employing his latest breath in kind attention to his friend, compared to your pretended Philosopher, who shuddered at the approaches of no early death, with an excess of pusillanimous horror, which has exposed him to a more apt comparison with the cowardly, effeminate Mecænas.

LADY CAROLINE.

A severe parallel, indeed! methodically drawn, and delivered with an oratorical vehemence that I never saw you assume before.—But, as I have exalted myself into a judicial office, let me imitate, my dear Colonel, the grand court of justice among your favourite Athenians (as those sapient judges always sate, I think, in the dark, you may

may allow me to be a little like them) and let me forbid all the delusive insinuations of impassioned eloquence.—I have still to request from you both, a few remarks on the style of your respective favourites.—The Archdeacon, I believe, esteems Johnson the very Sampson of language, as we lately heard him called by one of his more affected admirers.

THE ARCHDEACON.

Indeed, Madam, I think our language has infinite obligations to him; and the Colonel, who is a lover of spirit in every shape, can hardly prefer the loose and feeble phraseology of Chesterfield, or of Addison, to the compact vigour of our energetic Philologist.

THE COLONEL.

Though you may probably think me severely prejudiced against your favourite in some points, I trust you will not think so in the article of diction: for I allow that we find frequent passages in Johnson, where the amazing vigour of his expression is equalled by its beauty. I recollect, in his character of Dryden, a sentence that shews us the wonderful powers of his language. He there describes a tendency to talk nonsense, in such terms as render it an object of great sublimity. Do you remember the words? I think they run thus: " He delighted to tread upon
" the brink of meaning, where light
" and darkness begin to mingle; to
" approach the precipice of absurdity,
" and

"and hover over the abyss of unideal vacancy."—But there is an excellence which Johnson has very justly remarked in Dryden's language, and which he greatly wanted himself. The excellence I mean, he describes in a paragraph that I have transcribed in my memorandums, under the article we are speaking of. Here it is:

"His style could not easily be imitated, either seriously or ludicrously; for, being always equable, and always varied, it has no prominent or discriminative characters. The Beauty, who is totally free from disproportion of parts and features, cannot be ridiculed by an overcharged resemblance *."

* Life of Dryden.

If the excellence of language may be eſtimated by this ſtandard, that of Johnſon is aſſuredly very defective; for nothing is more eaſy than to execute a caricatura of his ſtyle. In reading him, we are frequently tempted to exclaim, as La Bruyere does on certain ſermons, O! what a rich figure is the antitheſis! it produces a whole Rambler. With a great command of words, he certainly wanted the noble and graceful ſimplicity which we admire in the capital writers of every country, from Homer, Plato, and Demoſthenes, down to that Addiſon, whom the partizans of your Philoſopher call a weak writer when compared to Johnſon; as there were once people in Rome, who preferred the eloquence of Seneca to that of Cicero.

The language of Chesterfield strikes me like a damsel in a fashionable morning dress of the most simple and captivating elegance. That of Johnson, is like a matron who has arrayed herself for some grand ceremonial, and heightened the austere dignity of her form, by all the rich stiffness of a flowery brocade.

If I were to compare the style of your Philosopher with that of Addison, I should say, that Johnson has the spirit, the grandeur, and the monotony of the kettle-drum; Addison, the rich variety of that sacred instrument, which can equally delight us with airy sweetness and awful solemnity. But as I am no connoisseur in the music of language, perhaps my idea is not so just as the opinion of some good-natured critics upon style, who, while they are rattling a salt-box themselves, have the kindness to tell their auditors, there is no strength or body in the tones of an organ.

Let me return to the diction of Chesterfield.—The best panegyric I can devise for it will be, to read you the following paragraph, addressed to him by your Philologist.

"I may hope, my Lord, that since
"you, whose authority in our language
"is so generally acknowledged, have
"commissioned me to declare my own
"opinion, I shall be considered as ex-
"ercising a kind of vicarious jurisdic-
"tion; and that the power which might
"have been denied to my own claim,
"will

"will be readily allowed me as the de-
"legate of your Lordſhip *."—You
will readily allow, my good friend, that
the man muſt have been no weak maſter in the ſcience of words, who could
extort ſuch a compliment from an author uncommonly ſparing of literary
courteſy to all living merit.—But I
will not launch out into new cenſures
on your idol. Indeed, as he has ſo frequently excited my ſpleen by his ſeverity towards various favourites of mine,
both in politics and poetry, I may poſ-
ſibly harbour prejudices againſt him,
almoſt as violent and cruel as his own—
you, I think, have as ſtrong a bias in
his favour, from your benevolent pre-
ſumption, that his real goodneſs was as

* Johnſon's Plan of an Engliſh Dictionary.

great as his oftentatious difplay of morality. But my fifter is a fort of neutral power, who may fairly fettle the difference between us; and I am fure you will join with me in requefting her to give us, I will not fay her judgment, for the word would alarm and terrify her diffidence, but her genuine feelings towards the two characters in queftion.

THE ARCHDEACON.

I join indeed moft heartily in your requeft; and beg leave, at the fame time, to remind Lady Caroline, that fhe is the true perfect judge, not only of moral but of literary merit, according to an honeft and candid fentiment of the mighty Critic himfelf; who fays, you know, in fpeaking with liberal praife of Gray's Elegy, "By the common fenfe
"of

"of readers, uncorrupted with literary
"prejudices, after all the refinements
"of subtilty, and the dogmatism of
"learning, must be finally decided all
"claim to poetical honours *."

LADY CAROLINE.

You are very good, to encourage me by such a quotation; but I really have not confidence enough to deliver any thing like a formal opinion upon characters of such eminence, even to you with whom I am so familiar. I do not mean, however, to shrink entirely from your request, which would, I think, be very unfair, after the entertainment that I have received from you both—and to pretend, that I have formed to myself no notions concerning two au-

* Life of Gray.

thors

thors whom you know I read very frequently, would be a foolish sort of prudery indeed: I shall tell you therefore, very frankly, how I have felt myself affected by your respective favourites. —To speak of them as men, I never felt in my life the slightest wish to have been personally acquainted with either; though in reading many authors, and Addison in particular, I have felt such a desire.—Johnson, I think, said to some young Lady, "Miss, I am a tame mon-"ster, you may stroke me." If he said so, for I do not recollect where I met with the anecdote, I apprehend his expression was not perfectly true.—He certainly was not more than half-tamed.—I do not believe that I could have been induced to give the fearless pat of friendly familiarity to either of these very opposite creatures. I am persuaded,

suaded, that my hand would have shrunk from Johnson, as from a hedge-hog; and from Chesterfield, if not as an adder too venomous to be touched, yet certainly as an eel too slippery to be held. For, notwithstanding my brother's panegyric on the friendly qualities of his idol, I cannot think that either he or the Philosopher had a heart truly formed for that tender connection. They seem to me to have possessed an equal degree of selfishness, though it shewed itself under very different shapes—one was continually trying to bully, and the other to inveigle the world into an exclusive admiration of his particular talents. The men accuse our sex of being actuated by a spirit of rivalship and mutual injustice to each other. Yet surely this is not only as visible among themselves,

themselves, but more productive of general disadvantage. What the Archdeacon observed of Johnson and Garrick, leads me to make a similar observation on Johnson and Chesterfield. Had these two men, of rare and different talents, instead of kindling into a contemptuous animosity, contracted a solid friendship, on the noble plan of honouring, of enjoying the perfections and correcting the deficiencies of each other, how infinitely might such conduct have contributed to the pleasure, improvement, happiness, and lasting glory of both! But the defects in each were too strong to let him derive all possible delight and advantage from the faculties of the other. Great as they both were in their separate lines, I cannot think that either was truly entitled to the epithet of amiable

able or good; for I am equally offended by truth that is delivered with brutality, and by politeness that is utterly insincere: I own myself as much an enemy to the splenetic malevolence of Johnson, as to the licentious vanity of Chesterfield. Could they have blended their better qualities; could the gaiety of the Wit have cured the spleen of the Philosopher; and, could the strong intellect of Johnson have annihilated the libertinism of Chesterfield, each might have been, what I think neither was, a truly accomplished and happy man: and each might have been rendered, by such a process, a more perfect and delightful writer; for, as it is, though we admire the wonderful understanding and energy of mind displayed by Johnson, though we are charmed by the wit, elegance, and knowledge

of

of the world, that we find in Chesterfield, yet it is certain that each fails us in the very point where, from his particular pursuits, we might naturally suppose it most safe to take him as a guide. The literary judgments of Johnson, and the worldly admonitions of Chesterfield, appear to me equally unsound. The first are, surely, not consistent with truth and justice;—and for the latter, I am afraid no apologist can perfectly reconcile them to honesty and virtue. Yet there is such a mass of real, though different excellence, united to the gross failings of those two authors, that, as a parent anxious to collect every thing that may render me useful to my children, I read them both with equal eagerness; and I find much innocent instruction in Chesterfield, that a mother's heart is inclined to adopt. Let rigid Moralists tell me, if they please, that all his parental merit is of the womanish kind; and that he is, at best,

Fine by defect, and delicately weak.

As to Johnson, I have indeed many jarring ideas of his excellencies and defects; yet, I believe, I may give you my notion of his character, comprized in a line, by which Pope has described the whole species. I shall conclude, therefore, by telling you, that he was, to my apprehension,

A Being darkly wise, and rudely great.

THE COLONEL.

Admirably applied!—You have expressed, in a single verse, what I laboured ed to say ineffectually, in a great deal of prose.—So adieu, for this morning.

THE ARCHDEACON.

Stay, Colonel!—do not leave us so hastily.

THE COLONEL.

I must be gone;—but I will not shut the door without remarking, that if Chesterfield had known our Lady, he would have thought better of women than he did; and if Johnson had possessed your true christian virtues, my dear Doctor, he would have been a much happier being than he was.—So farewell.

FINIS.